The Kindness
of a
STRANGER

James Ruddy

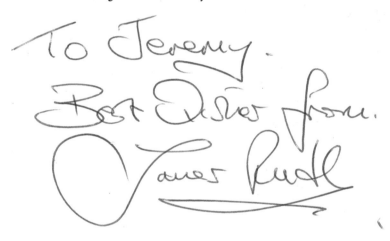

*To Jeremy.
Best Wishes from.
James Rudd*

THE ERSKINE PRESS
1999

The Kindness of a Stranger – James Ruddy

First published in 1999 by
The Erskine Press
The Old Bakery, Banham, Norwich, Norfolk NR16 2HW

Text © James Ruddy 1999
This edition © The Erskine Press 1999
Photographs © Eastern Daily Press

ISBN 1 85297 057 X

Typeset by Waveney Typesetters
Wymondham, Norfolk

Printed in Great Britain by
M. F. Barnwell & Sons
Aylsham, Norfolk

CONTENTS

Introduction – A Very Ordinary Man		v
Foreword		vii
Preface		ix
The Beginning		1
I	If We Break Down Now We're Dead	4
	North-Eastern Croatia – December 1992	
II	It Was Cold And Dark Behind The Blast Curtains	16
	Sarajevo – January 1994	
III	Then The Serbs Came	35
	Operation Mostar – March 1994	
Interlude – Stoke-on-Trent		43
Interlude – Norfolk		46
IV	It Started Routinely Enough	52
	Sarajevo Diary – March 1995	
Interlude – A Concert		81
V	A Soldier's Life	89
	Rapid Reaction Force – September 1995	
VI	He Must Have Been A Brave Man	106
	Sarajevo – December 1995	
VII	No-One Knew Her Real Name, So They Called Her Tenneh	119
	Freetown, Sierra Leone– May 1996	
Interlude – Norwich		124
VIII	Ambush Alley	127
	Freetown, Sierra Leone – 1996	
IX	The Orphans Left In The Night	139
	Freetown, Sierra Leone – December 1998	
Epilogue		146
A Letter From Freetown		152
With Thanks		154

INTRODUCTION

A VERY ORDINARY MAN

On a recent visit to our homes in Romania I came across the family home of Elie Wiesel. He experienced the true horrors of war in Auschwitz and went on to win the Nobel Peace Prize. At the opening of the Holocaust Museum in Washington he said, *'Indifference is a sin and a punishment. When we see people suffer we cannot remain indifferent'*.

I believe the world is made up of good, bad and indifferent people. Most of us fall into the latter category. Travelling around war and disaster zones, I have met some wonderful people and others who are truly evil. Wars bring out the best and worst in those who get caught up in them; deeds of incredible bravery and humanity compete with acts of unbelievable barbarity. Soldiers are trained for war and most hope to experience all the emotions that go with it, at least once in their lives. Once is normally enough.

But the recent war in the Balkans was different for most of us living in this country, whether we were directly involved in it or not. Night after night we saw people like our own relatives and next door neighbours being killed and maimed and little children being orphaned and made homeless. How can this be allowed to happen? Why doesn't somebody do something to stop it? For most, the questions have no answer and so their concern ends. However, for some there is another question, *'What can I do to help those who are suffering?'* Because of the intense media coverage this conflict pricked the conscience of many like no other. If anything can be salvaged from the carnage, then let us cease to be indifferent to those who suffer.

James Ruddy, as the deputy editor of the country's biggest regional newspaper, the *Eastern Daily Press*, had no reason whatsoever to get involved in what was going on in Croatia and Bosnia – it was a long way and very remote from all the parochial problems of Norfolk. However, something happened which was to change his life.

He introduces himself as 'a very ordinary man', until the bubble of his complacency was pierced. He might have been ordinary before but by the time you have finished the book you will realise that he is not now. He went out to see for himself what was going on, not only as a journalist but as a man of compassion and as a father with a wife and two children.

His vivid, first-hand accounts of what was happening in Croatia and Bosnia and then in Sierra Leone must have burst many bubbles in East Anglia. *Eastern Daily Press* readers have responded generously in support of various aid programmes and over the last seven years James has helped countless people in various ways, proving that *'the pen is mightier than the sword'*.

Sadly, those who lose most because of our inhumanity are children and, being a father, James has shown a particular desire to help them. Caroline and I are extremely grateful for his interest and support since we staffed Hope and Homes for Children, which has the specific aim of providing homes for the innocent young victims of war or disaster. We now have more supporters in East Anglia than anywhere else and I doubt that we would be active in eight countries had it not been for his personal involvement. He has been on many visits with us to ensure that funds are spent properly and he has often put his life at risk to help others.

In 1992 James Ruddy's 'bubble of complacency' was pierced by a child. It was his own daughter, Janna aged 5, who asked 'Why can't you do anything to help, Daddy?'

He answered her question in a most marvellous way and, when she grows up, she will be very proud of him.

February 1999   MARK COOK

FOREWORD

While many may not have perceived that the calling of a newspaper reporter is a noble one, at one time the reporter and the paper for whom he worked were trusted by the readership. Sadly, in recent times, the media and, in particular, the press, has been the subject of close scrutiny by the public and generally found wanting. In part, journalism has suffered much the same fate as the other professions in its loss of public esteem and, in part, the wound has been self-inflicted. This is certainly true of the national press but not so the local papers who by and large have escaped much of the opprobrium. This is due in no small part to reporters like James Ruddy, who have retained their integrity and standards. They continue to present the local news and affairs of the community in which they live honestly and fairly and have over time earned the trust and respect of their readership.

James Ruddy is a deputy editor of the *Eastern Daily Press* and writes features for the paper in the field of human interest. Latterly his articles have tended to focus on civil wars and the damage they inflicted on the local population, firstly in Bosnia and then in Sierra Leone. It was in this context that we first met in the spring of 1996 to discuss Tenneh Cole and her medical problems. I had become wary of the press, having been misquoted on a number of occasions whilst serving as a member of a health authority, and so I was somewhat cautious. My fears were ungrounded; the article which he wrote was objective, precise and accurate – hallmarks I came to associate with him. The effect his first account of this little girl's story had on the people of Norfolk and beyond was extraordinary – to judge by the media attention it received. I only became aware that the report had spread world-wide when my son-in-law 'phoned to say that he had read it in the English version of the *South China News* whilst eating his breakfast in Shanghai the following day. This was due in no small measure to the unsentimental yet compassionate account which James had written of her plight.

The story has not stopped there but continues with accounts of the child and her companions in the orphanage at Makeni coping in the face of the continuing civil strife. Throughout this unhappy saga, James' humanity and concern for these unfortunate children shines through and for this we should all be grateful.

February 1999   GEOFFREY CHENEY
                                      Consultant Oral & Maxillo Facial Surgeon

PREFACE

'Welcome brother James to the house of peace and love,
Welcome brother James to our home . . .'

I could hear the children singing when the pick-up truck was still half a mile from the orphanage.

It was that rich *mélange* of voices so familiar anywhere you go in Africa. There was clapping too. And backing them was that velvety bass of their Uncle Joseph, the gentle giant with the huge smile and effusive humour.

As we wheeled into the sun-baked compound, the clapping choir was gathered in front of the granite boulders, with Joseph acting as cheerleader and conductor.

As soon as the dust began to settle, I stepped out and saw her, Tenneh, the girl whose name meant 'God will provide' and whom the world had called 'A Walking Miracle'. She was clapping too, and her mouth was trying to voice the words she could not hear of a song she did not know.

The Danavox hearing aid had been discarded in a fit of anger. But she looked happy, alongside her best friend, Amie Jabatti, the tiny figure in a pink dress who had shown her so much love.

Within seconds of the engine stopping, the children broke ranks and ran towards me, still singing and clapping, some tripping and falling, others skipping and laughing.

It had been four months since I had returned Tenneh to Sierra Leone, her West African homeland.

There had been doubts about her future in a country where regular military coups accompanied by slaughter and corruption make it one of the three poorest in the world.

Why, I had been asked, did I fly this young girl to England for a life-saving operation to remove a bullet from her brain and then take her back to such a place?

The answers were many and complex. I retold them many times for the television and radio interviewers. But there would always be doubts.

Now, I knew it had been the correct decision. Her hearing had already been damaged by the meningitis following the initial bullet wound, which meant she had great difficulty coping during her stay in England.

Despite the care and love showered upon her, the culture, the experiences, the whole roller coaster ride had been a bewildering trauma for an orphan girl who had already witnessed untold horrors in the bush war and the refugee camps.

Now, in the compound of the new children's home in Makeni, I saw her again. Clapping. Trying to sing. Laughing at the muffled sounds of her friends' singing. A child among children. This was where she belonged. Not among strangers in a strange land.

As the children leapt at me, pulling my shirt, my shorts, small hands squeezing my own, she stood back, in her proud, defiant way, still clapping and humming, refusing to acknowledge me. Perhaps, I thought, I was just one of those strangers now. A reminder of an episode, like so many in her short life, that she would prefer to forget.

I was wrong. Not for the first time about Tenneh. She bided her time and when the others had calmed down and I was eating bread and drinking a cup of tea made by Uncle Joseph, she sneaked up behind me and placed a hand upon mine; squeezed, then ran away, laughing the laugh of mischief.

This was Tenneh the proud one. Tenneh, the girl whom, the odds had decreed, should really have been dead. But also Tenneh the girl whose thirst for life had given her a future.

Little did I know how that future would again be threatened and how Uncle Joseph and others would be consumed by the terror that was just round the corner ...

THE BEGINNING

I am a very ordinary man and have found myself swept up in extraordinary events.

The trigger was pulled in 1992, when the awfulness of the war in former Yugoslavia began to fill our television screens and newspapers. Like so many people, I felt helpless, unable to do what was needed to protect the innocent. Governments were failing the mothers in rags who we saw, hugging those small children, as they trudged along the roads in their thousands, fleeing their once-idyllic Balkan towns and villages that had become smoking ruins.

As a father of two children I became increasingly frustrated at the plight of those who had no control over their destiny. My own children's questions were one of the catalysts for action. My daughter Janna, then aged five, asked me one day, with a child's innocence: 'Why can't you do anything to help, daddy?'

It was to be a turning point in my life. It pierced the bubble of my complacency. Why could I not do something? I who had always prided myself on possessing a modest level of original thought and assertiveness. How could I ignore such a cry from the heart of one so young?

I had never been driven by selflessness or any self-enforced requirement to do good in the world. My Roman Catholic prep school education in a Lincolnshire convent had provided me with a solid grounding in the value of charity, humility and kindness. All had been delivered by the sisters of the Order of the Poor Clares through a confusing mixture of gentle persuasion and regular blows from a heavy wooden ruler.

But my chosen path of journalism has brought me into contact with enough duplicity, selfishness and cruelty to foster a distinct layer of cynicism within me. Scratch the surface of most people, though, and I am convinced you will find the flame of goodness flickering away. All that is needed is a catalyst to move them sufficiently and a conduit through which they can deliver their kindness.

The Yugoslavian civil war was the fuel for the fire. And I soon discovered that my newspaper, the *Eastern Daily Press*, would be a ready vehicle. As a regional morning newspaper with around 220,000 readers, the title had long been recognised for its charity appeals, mostly helping to plug gaping holes in local services. Child abuse response teams and emergency radios for ambulances were among subjects that had inspired people to raise many thousands of pounds.

It was no surprise that these were successful: East Anglians are renowned for looking after their own. But Yugoslavia was a different proposition. These were people with exotic ethnic descriptions such as Serb, Croat and Bosnian, whose nationalist aspirations had been suppressed by the iron hand of Tito's federal security forces for more than four decades. Now their bewildering struggles for separate destinies had created a cauldron of death and destruction in their once-orderly and beautiful land. Their plight struck a chord with East Anglians, and not just because of the media images. It was also because thousands of them had flown to Yugoslavia before the fighting for package trips in what had been regarded as a safe and secure destination from the provincial Norwich Airport. Dubrovnik, Split and Mostar had been on the holiday circuit. Now they were caught up in an incomprehensible fight to the death involving leaders with unpronounceable names, flying flags with unfamiliar symbols. And most of the victims were innocent men, women and children.

As a result, those warm and generous East Anglians responded magnificently. They came up with hundreds of tonnes of food, blankets, clothes and other carefully chosen winter supplies. In the years which have followed, they have poured money and aid donations into efforts across Croatia, Bosnia and Sierra Leone, the West African country which has also been devastated by civil war.

Some of those missions of hope have made world headlines. In 1994, using that support, I helped organise and joined the first British surgical team to fly into besieged Sarajevo, where innocents were dying every day under a hail of artillery and sniper fire.

The following year, in Mostar, where an estimated 20,000 civilians were killed, I helped set up the evacuation of twelve sick and badly injured children to the UK for medical treatment. At the same time, I was able to arrange for £20,000 to be used to launch the charity Hope and Homes for Children. Then, in 1996, I was asked by the charity to help bring seven-year-old orphan, Tenneh Cole from Sierra Leone to the UK for surgery to remove a bullet from her brain. The following year I was also able to fulfil a promise to Britain's then foreign aid minister Lady Chalker to send seventeen tonnes of toys to the children of Sarajevo, where we had helped Hope and Homes for Children to rebuild the city's war-shattered main orphanage.

Each time, I have made a point of travelling into the war zones, ensuring the aid has been properly delivered and has reached those in greatest need. At times, I have wondered what I was doing there. Pinned down by a sniper in Sarajevo or hiding in a restaurant with shells rocking the streets outside, I have promised myself that this time would be the last.

But then I have seen the orphans, sleeping securely in their beds in rebuilt rooms in the children's home in Sarajevo. Or I have felt the small, warm hands reach out to clasp mine in the compound in Sierra Leone. Then I have known that this is how life should be – not simply a pursuit of that next holiday in the sun, an index-linked pension and a warm pair of slippers in front of the television.

Every father has a responsibility to his own children. Sometimes I have had a nagging feeling that not dying young ought to be counted among them. But there is also a need to show them that the modern world *really is* a global village in which the rich have obligations to help the poor and the desperate.

It may seem a foolish and naive proposition. It has certainly felt, sometimes, that we have been used and abused in our efforts to try and shed a little light in so many dark places.

But children remain our future. I see it in my own son and daughter as I grow older and they grow stronger and wiser. Through all my frailties, I try not to make mistakes that they will learn to regret. Like so many parents, I try to show them a road that is worth following, in a small, modest way. And, in a world that is often hard, often cruel, I try to show them they should never fear the hurt they may find from opening their hearts to those in need.

If this book reveals anything, I hope it illustrates that it lies in the hearts of many people to bring themselves to show the kindness of a stranger to those they may never know.

Over the past six years, if I have learned one lesson from the cruelty and compassion I have witnessed, it is this: a tiny offering can provide a world of hope to a child without love.

I would like to dedicate this book to those children of war who have felt the true kindness of a stranger.

August 1998   JAMES RUDDY

I

IF WE BREAK DOWN NOW WE'RE DEAD

North-Eastern Croatia, December 1992

If we break down now we're dead. If we stop for any reason, we're dead. We have to keep moving. Just keep your fingers crossed …'

It was a starlit and freezing night. The words were urgent and clipped, delivered in the harsh tones of the English Midlands. They were uttered by a specialist UN British Army driver. I was riding alongside him in an ageing ambulance donated by a private medical group.

We were passing through a zone of total destruction. There were no people, only burned-out villages, streets covered with rubble, bullet-riddled villas, rusting cars, eerie silence.

An occasional fox peered furtively from behind a fir tree, eyes glowing like silver specks in the beam from our headlights. Lop-eared rabbits scurried across the twisting mountain road, as the diesel engine roared at full power through that dramatic karst limestone countryside filled with sharp peaks and roaring streams, slicing white, foaming scars across the darkly, wooded slopes.

Its beauty and peace had once attracted so many affluent German and Italian visitors. They had stayed in its alpine villages, dined in its famed roadside restaurants, walked and climbed its pine-forested crags, and taken the cure of its famed spa waters.

Now those villages were deathly quiet. Their Croatian inhabitants had fled or died during the maelstrom of slaughter which had swept through them in the previous year. The hated Serbian Chetniks had poured in from the south and east. Backed by the largely Serb Yugoslav National Army (JNA), these indisciplined fanatics had shot, looted and burned almost everything in their path in their drive to control this disputed zone on the fault line between Serbia and Croatia.

And they were still out there. In the darkness. Waiting for a rare vehicle

4

French UN armoured vehicle, Sarajevo 1995

An orphan in his shattered bedroom, Sarajevo 1995

The old bridge at Mostar

Aerial view of ethnic cleansing, near Mostar 1994

The new bridge over the river Neretva, Mostar 1994

Sleeping rough, Sarajevo 1995

Shotgun victim, Admir Vele, in the Norfolk and Norwich Hospital, Christmas 1994

to slow down or stop. They had left their calling cards on the sides of buildings, the Serbian Cross or Ovo Je Srbija (This is Serbia) scrawled in black Cyrillic script.

We knew that they could pounce without warning. If they set up a night roadblock, they would not be seeking conversation. My driver's UN blue beret would be regarded as a trophy rather than as a symbol of peace. We knew we would have to try to smash through. The white, thin skinned ambulance would make an easy target for their high velocity weapons. The bullets would riddle its sides like a colander. Our ageing reconditioned engine would hardly allow us to outrun them. It was a grim prospect, which neither of us had wanted to discuss.

Since swinging off the main road at the small town of Novska, we had immediately passed through the final checkpoint. The two Croatian policemen there had shrugged without optimism when we had inquired about our chances of survival on that road in the failing light.

It had been our last contact with what had resembled civilisation. Now we had entered a bubble that was labelled on military planners' maps as the disputed Pakrac pocket. Euphemistically nominated a UN-Controlled Zone, it was home to roving bands of killers. Here UN troops had been numbered among the dead, even their heavy-tracked, armoured personnel carriers had been blown up by mines along the road. These blue-helmeted soldiers had also been known to make what they described as 'the twenty metre leap' after touching the many booby traps that littered the area.

The prospects were not good. In a land without law, we were acutely aware there was little to prevent the renegades from killing us, stealing what food and valuables we might have, then moving on to their next point of plunder.

We had been driving for over nine hours, heading for the small spa town of Lipik which had received some of the twelve juggernaut loads of emergency aid donated by *Eastern Daily Press* readers. I wanted to record how the aid had been used and the views of the people who had received it. Most of all, I wanted to see the orphans who had been blasted out of their home in Lipik. In a war that had so many complexities, the one truism was that the innocent young were the most tangible victims. At home, many people had become bewildered by the agendas of the fighting factions. But everyone had understood that children were dying on all sides. And that they needed help.

I was certain that the people who had donated so much aid deserved to know their food and other supplies had been well used.

The deliveries had been made by Alan Waller, who ran a health and fitness shop in Norwich. Compact and powerful, he was something of an enigma; a bachelor in his mid-twenties who described himself as an ex-US

Marine and ex–British paratrooper, Alan had left his shop and had been making the drops voluntarily for some months from a warehouse at Krk, on a peaceful stretch of Croatia's south coast. He was driving in convoy with us in his red Toyota Hi-Lux, accompanied by photographer Simon Finlay who, like me, was making his first trip into a war zone.

The ambulance had been donated and loaded onto our latest lorryload of aid. It was heading for Lipik to provide a lifeline for the doctor in the devastated town.

The past fifteen kilometres of that tortuous journey had seemed like an eternity. Staring sharply at every movement caught in the headlights, my heart had been pulsing hard in my temples. We had just passed the halfway point along this road when we rounded a bend near Brezovac and my worst fears were confirmed.

Beside me, the driver suddenly sucked in a lungful of breath and went into a routine for which he was clearly trained. The ambulance slowed sharply. Off went the headlights. On again. Off again. And they stayed off.

'Don't move,' he ordered, a note of charged authority in the voice. 'Don't say anything. Don't do anything. If I give you an order, just follow it …'

I squinted at the scene ahead of us. Without the lights, I could make out several figures, some standing, some lying on the ground spaced at either side of their roadblock. All were pointing long dark objects at us. Any chance of escape was gone.

As we ambled slowly forward, more definition grew in the darkness. A light at the roadblock picked out a flag. Then the uniforms. The helmets. Then the sign: STOP: UN CONTROL.

Ahead of us a collection of UN Jordanian troops remained behind their sandbags, gripping their heavy machine guns and automatic rifles. As we stopped, the driver stepped out and identified himself. The soldiers' relief was almost ecstatic. This was not like any other UN post we had encountered. The small, polite troops from the desert kingdom were shivering in the freezing Balkan night air. Of all the UN detachments, they had suffered most from the climate, ordering extra thermal clothing and equipment since their deployment. At first it appeared the whole checkpoint had been shivering at our approach, foggy breath rising from their dugouts. Their demeanour eased slightly at the recognition of a friend and not a vehicle loaded with bearded Chetniks looking for a firefight.

Yet they did not release their trigger fingers, as their officer, in polished Sandhurst-tones, greeted us warmly and expressed his surprise at seeing such a vehicle travelling at night along such a road.

'It is not a good situation,' he advised us with some irony, fingering an exquisite moustache and smiling broadly. 'Make sure you do not stop. You may regret doing so.'

As we pulled away, he waved without smiling, his face betraying the look of someone who felt he might not be seeing us again.

It was after 10 o'clock when we reached Lipik. Even in the shadows the level of its destruction was unmitigated. Our lights picked out the bullet-riddled town sign, hanging limply near a shell crater. Then we passed down what seemed to be the main street, where every building had been raked by gunfire of different calibres. It was as if Roald Dahl's giant had turned unfriendly and rampaged through the whole place. Clearly, this was a classic case of what the UN called 'town trashing'. After the initial artillery bombardment by Serbian heavy weapons mostly owned previously by the JNA, the Chetniks would move in to quash any resistance, with tanks and mortars destroying every Croat-owned building in a systematic ethnic cleansing routine. The philosophy was based on the premise that a people ousted from their homes would always threaten to retake them, unless they no longer existed. In some cases, as in Lipik, a counter-attack by Croatia's burgeoning national forces had wrested the town back, with Serb-owned buildings being destroyed with equally systematic precision.

The result was near-complete devastation. Almost every window was without glass, every villa roofless; even the big department store looked like a heap of children's toy bricks. Nearby, the church was a definitive pile of rubble, its heavy bell prostrate. And eerily, not a light could be seen in this town of apparent ghosts.

Then, as we swung the ambulance and the Hi-Lux right at the main crossroads, we noticed signs of life at the relatively intact Jura's cafe. First two middle-aged men came out mouthing greetings. Then, an ageing Yugo estate car spluttered into view, slewed to a halt and out leapt a small, black-haired woman sporting a white doctor's coat and a huge smile.

'Alan, oh Alan, you have come again,' she shouted, leaping at the muscular aid deliverer and squeezing him tightly.

'I am sorry I was not here to greet you straight away,' she said, hugging and kissing each of us in turn. 'I had a problem to attend to and must go back before I can be with you.'

The problem turned out to have involved Darko, a local man who had driven into a lamppost. It was the least of his worries, it emerged later, as his body was still sporting the seven machine gun bullets he had received in the bitter fighting in the town.

Like a whirlwind she had come. Now she turned to go again. Then her round, pretty face turned, her large dark eyes widened at the sight of our white vehicle, with its red stripe.

'Oh,' she cried. 'I forget, the ambulancia, how wonderful. You have brought it to me. With this ambulance-car I will start saving lives straight away. I thank you, thank you …'

With that she turned, slid into the spluttering Yugo and was gone, back up the rubble-strewn road and into the night.

Her departure brought an odd feeling of isolation and tension. Doubts about our safety had nagged at me since we had landed on that flight from Geneva in the Croatian capital, Zagreb. Journalists, we knew, were prized targets in this war. Twenty-two had been killed in the first nine months of the fighting and four had gone missing, presumed dead. Some had been killed accidentally by driving over mines. Many had been deliberately targeted by all sides. Some Serb leaders, in fact, were rumoured to be offering a reward of $200 on the heads of every journalist accounted for. Such was their fear of anyone daring to seek out the truth.

Rumour and propaganda were the daily diet of this conflict. So too were tension and uncertainty at what lay ahead.

For no logical reason I began to recall our first damp day in the grimly grey sprawl that was Zagreb. I had left the photographer, Simon, at the Intercontinental Hotel to hunt for an available telephone, and I had narrowly escaped death in comical circumstances. The great urban sprawl had largely escaped the fighting, apart from early clashes around the airport and other strategic points. We knew the Serb forces had been threatening to hit the city with heavy, ground-launched missiles from beyond the front line, sixty kilometres south. But no-one appeared to be taking them seriously. Until I stepped onto a four-lane boulevard alongside the hotel and felt the ground shake from a huge and not-too-distant explosion.

A car, the only car in sight on that damp morning, which had been passing along the inside lane, swerved toward me. Its driver, a middle-aged man wearing a flat, grey cap had clearly panicked at the blast. One of those moments of inertia struck me as the engine roared and reality dawned. I jumped clear, rolling on the carriageway and coming to rest with my face tingling against the coldness of a shiny tramline. I looked up and saw the car screaming past, still swerving, tyres squealing as it went. Nursing a few bruises I let out a chuckle of relief when I described the incident later to Simon. Married, in his twenties and with a wry sense of humour, he saw the immediate irony: 'Just think how that would have looked. You, wiped out by a car accident on a city street, on your very first day in a war zone. Not a good idea. Not good at all.'

That had happened forty-eight hours earlier. Yet it had seemed like an eternity. The mysterious Alan had not shown up in Zagreb as planned. He was totally out of contact. We decided to take the train south to Rijeka and then a bus to the island of Krk where we knew he rented rooms from a Serb refugee family and maintained the aid warehouse. The uncertainty had added to the tension. But we had finally met up with him, stayed the night and picked up the Army driver and ambulance for the trip to Lipik.

Now we had arrived, I felt relief that we would be able to record some interviews with people who had been helped by the generosity of those at home. But there was also a distinct air of menace around us.

As we stood in the cold night and surveyed the scene in the lights from the cafe, it resembled a demolition site. At least two families in a heavily damaged tenement block appeared to be hanging on. Their televisions were flickering behind sackcloth curtains, fed by aerials that dangled from glassless windows. I could hear a child chuckle. Then I heard a distinctive rattle in the distance.

'What was that?' I asked a large man in a check shirt who had stepped out of the cafe to greet us.

'Just rabbit shooting,' he assured me, waving a hand dismissively. 'Nothing but rabbit shooting.'

It was the type of understatement and disinformation which I was to encounter regularly over the coming days. Commonsense told me that no-one went rabbit shooting with a machine gun. Not even in a place where everyone seemed to carry a firearm and many looked ready to use it at the slightest provocation.

Inside the bar, the strong Karlovaci beer, which had somehow made its way there, helped to dampen our concerns.

The young owner, we were told, was a pretty Serb girl who had stayed behind to tend the wounded when her countrymen had first attacked in the summer of the previous year. After the initial wave of shelling and mortar fire from the surrounding hills there had been the classic lull in the assault. This opened the way for terrified residents to flee, sometimes into ambushes, sometimes to refugee camps after a long and tortuous journey. All that had remained in Lipik were thirty-five men and women prepared to stand and fight to hold off the advancing Serbs until help from Croatian forces or the UN arrived. And she had been among them, defending her own town against her own ethnic kind.

Now, with most of that small group dead or wounded, the Serbs had been forced out, only to return and be forced out once again by the Croats, leaving the UN to keep the sides apart. The girl was back at the bar, laughing and joking with her few customers. Most were men in farming jeans and shirts who spoke in deep, determined tones, their heavy eyes darting towards the door and windows at the sound of the occasional burst of firing in the dank night outside. Many had placed their Kalashnikovs, hunting rifles and automatic revolvers on the tables or the wooden bar top itself.

The atmosphere was what you would have imagined in one of those frontier towns in America's Wild West. Most of its remaining people, even under the influence of huge quantities of Karlovaci and that fiery Yugoslavian clear spirit, Slivovic, appeared ready to fight and die if the 'indians' returned to town. And leading them was their tiny power pack of a doctor, Marina Topic.

During the next three days, I was to christen her the Angel of Lipik. Her raw courage in helping save the wounded at the height of the fighting was related to me by several people. She had come close to death numerous times, carrying patched up broken bodies in her Yugo, down the deadly road to nearby Pakrac hospital. Rockets and bullets had splattered along the carriageway around her, but still she had driven on, again and again, in a near-fatalistic crusade to fulfil her role as the town's only physician.

Her motivation was an explosive hatred of everything Serbian. Ironically, she had married a Serb doctor. It had been the right thing for a Croat to do before the war. But the union ended in divorce after a difficult pregnancy and the death of their only son Ivan a few weeks after his birth. Now she was alone in a town that was clinging to survival.

When she returned to the cafe, she breezed in with apologies, smiling, kissing us all, inviting us to her apartment for the night. Her home was in a dark and sinister apartment block, largely uninhabited. She had battled to restore its kitchen and living room into a comfortable base. And one of the first items she showed us was the tail fin of a rocket.

'This is my paperweight,' she explained. 'It was the rocket which the Chetniks fired through the window when they were killing and destroying Lipik. I keep it as a souvenir. Everything has some use and it reminds me of them.

'If they come back we will fight them again. We will rebuild again, like we have done this time. They will never defeat us. We are a nation again and we will remain a nation forever.'

The words brought a wateriness to her large dark eyes and a reddening of her small, oval face. It was not a speech. Just a statement of fact from a woman whose fervour seemed to be boundless.

As she made us a meal with her few provisions and arranged our sleeping places, it was clear she was also a woman in turmoil. Over the coming days I was to discover precisely why.

Her apartment was just across the field from the front line. There lay the dreaded Bosnian Serb Chetniks, who had caused so much destruction, waiting, calculating the benefits of another attack. Her life, like so many in that haunted place, was hanging on a slender thread. Even worse, I also learned, she was suffering a serious skin disease which was threatening to consume her. It was a key reason for her need to achieve much in what might be a very short life.

Her supporters and admirers were many. Volatile and self-willed, she was a classic example of that Yugoslavian cocktail which blends extreme kindness for friends with the deepest hatred of a perceived enemy. Like an emotional chameleon, in the same breath she could express her sensitivity for those in need and immediately call down destruction and damnation on the Serbs.

It was shortly after we first met that the passions she aroused were underlined. A British soldier took me aside into the damp and dark corridor of her front line apartment block, and issued a warning that was hard to ignore.

'I am pleased you and Simon are doing what you are doing here,' he whispered. 'But just get one thing straight. If you write anything bad about her, anything, then I'll kill you both. Wherever you are, whenever it is, I'll get to you and I'll shoot you. And that's a promise.' Then he went, leaving me wondering where the next threat would come from in this forsaken place.

It was with a troubled mind that I tried to sleep that first night. The quiet darkness was punctuated by the occasional single shot and burst of return fire in the distance. It was something I would come to read and recognise in the years to come. But that night it was hard to rest in the knowledge that a short distance away, someone was trying to kill someone else. Simon, his cameras boxed safely next to his prostrate body, and our Army driver appeared shattered by the day's events. They were in a deep slumber. Alan had gone to stay with some friends nearby. And later, as I got up for a glass of water from the kitchen, I was shocked to find Marina was sleeping on the cold, hard floor, having given up her bed and sofas to her guests. It was typical of the selfless gestures which had brought her adoration from her people.

Over the next three days, we witnessed how she worked her magic on so many of them. Like a child, she burst with excitement as we showed her round the ambulance and unloaded the medical supplies we had packed on board for her small surgery. We saw it again when she arranged for a dinner to be held in our honour. It was clear that these people had very little and they were giving their honoured guests what they could. Regaling us in front of the forty or so citizens who attended, she knew how to manipulate an event to the delight of those present. As we were shown around, we saw the pitiful half dozen tins of sardines on the shelves of the local shop, which had been reopened. In a secure store, we saw the blankets, sleeping bags and baby boxes of high value food which our people had sent and which had saved so many lives over the long months

11

in which the townspeople had battled for survival. Proudly, two civic leaders presented me with two green bottles of spa water from the reopened bottling plant.

And everywhere we saw the destruction upon which Marina had founded her determination to rebuild and revive the spirit of her beloved home and country.

In daylight, Lipik looked even worse than on that first night. On a tour she showed us the shell-shattered hospital, the hotel where wealthy tourists had taken the fabled 'cure' of its waters, and the Fontana, a once-elegant fountain in a beautiful formal garden. Set in a precise geometrical pattern, it contained the Kursalon, which was the pride of Lipik, with a concert hall, wooden dance floors and restaurants. Now it was riddled with shell holes, its roof crushed, its delicate glasswork shattered. Alan, the ex-soldier, explained with some fascination the difference between tank damage and that made by rockets, artillery and mortars. At one window, we saw hundreds of bullet marks in the crumbling plaster. Here, we were told, one of the thirty-five brave militiamen had made his last stand. Inside was an ugly, dark stain on the floor where he had died.

I shivered at the thought of the final moments of that husband or son fighting to the last against the swarm of killers, armed to the teeth, who were turning his home to rubble, raping and killing his friends and relatives.

Everywhere there were similar scenes of destruction. Marina told us how the Serbs had swept in.

Her voice quivered with anger and frustration as she told the story:

'This was a beautiful place before the war. It was admired throughout Europe. People came and enjoyed our waters, hospitality, luxury. There were fine walks in the mountains, fine food in the restaurants, the fields were fertile and people lived a good life.

'Now we have this. Nothing but death and destruction. But we have driven them out and we would kill them again if they came back.

'All around us we can see the fields where the people farmed their crops. They are now held by the Serbs and we cannot take them back because the UN protects them on *our* land.

'There is no justice in this war. Just hatred, defiance. We will take back what is ours, eventually. It is our right. The Chetniks will not have it. Why should they?'

When we reached the children's home a little further on, her anger became deeper; her arms waving, left and right, her eyes again welling up with tears. She spoke with a faltering voice.

'This place had stood for over a hundred years, a home for thousands of children in need. But now it is a shell, completely destroyed, its children forced out by the evil of men.

'It was the first place to be hit when the Chetniks came. The first shell smashed into the roof and the children were taken to the basement, screaming and crying in fear.

'There were thirty-five of them, many were very young, but they knew what the Serbs had been doing. They knew they had been killing and raping and destroying in the towns and villages. And now it was their turn …'

Her voice broke again at the memory.

The children had stayed for the ten days of the bombardment in the cellar, which had already been prepared for a siege. Some were sick and terrified. The staff were convinced they would be slaughtered when the Serbs broke through.

'The Serbs were raping and killing everywhere. Men, women and children, it did not matter to them,' Marina told us.

'The staff knew they had to get them out of there. If they had been discovered they would have been attacked and mutilated before being killed or just wiped out by grenades thrown through the windows.

'So Goran, the director, evacuated them in a coach and took them to safety in Bjelovar, where they lived at the school.'

After a month there, the first bombardment of Lipik petered out, as the Serbs moved on, looking for further, possibly easier, targets. The children were moved back to the orphanage. But within two days the shells began to explode in the town once more.Up to a thousand explosions were counted in one day, as the children spent the next eleven days back in the cellar. This time, the town was left with just these few men with hunting rifles and grenades to hold back the assaulting Chetniks.

Goran again organised an evacuation. The children were loaded screaming into a sandbagged lorry and driven west to Kutina under the noses of the Serb snipers and artillerymen in the hills.

On an exposed section of road they braved a hail of mortar fire and then passed the stables of the famous white Lippizaner horses, which perform at the riding school in Vienna.

They saw that the stables were burning and the horses were running around in a crazed state. As they pulled up sharply to avoid the animals, a rocket flew behind the lorry and another skimmed under a car ahead of them. It was a narrow escape. As they arrived in Kutina, thirty kilometres away, the children were hysterical. Behind them Lipik was in flames and the Serbs poured in, killing and destroying everything Croatian in their path.

That evacuation had been a miracle. The children, now numbering more than eighty, had been taken to another home on the south coast at Selse.

'My dream,' said Marina, throwing up her arms in the ruins of the orphanage, 'is that this will be rebuilt. We will bring the children back. It is a symbol for the world. They are children from across the divide, Croat, Serb, Bosnian, Hungarian. Children who know how it is to live together in peace.'

I was convinced then that her words were not hollow. They were spoken by a determined woman who would fulfil her mission against the odds. Throughout our days with her, we learned from others how close she had come to death during the assaults on Lipik. Her car had been rocketed. She had worked in filthy basements, under fire, on townspeople with appalling injuries. And despite her strength, her zeal and manipulative charisma, she remained bewilderingly vulnerable.

It was typical of her nature that she would not come with us when we said we would be making the long drive south to Selse to see the orphans.

As we were leaving, I thanked her and she held my arms tightly, her dark eyes burning with intensity. 'James, you know I cannot come because I have work to do here among my people. We will rebuild our town again and our children's home. As long as there is life in my body, I promise you that.'

The following day, at the children's home, we delivered a holdall filled with chocolate to the orphans. They accepted the sweets politely, their faces and their words sometimes expressing confusion at our gesture. Each of them who spoke told how they wanted to go home to Lipik, despite the horrors they had witnessed. 'It is our home where we wish to be happy again,' said one small boy, a Croat. His other wish was to play football for the leading Serbian team, Red Star Belgrade.

We all knew that their future was already decided. A brave young doctor who was fighting for her own life would ensure that they would have another chance at life.

Seven long and unnerving days after we had arrived at Zagreb, we bade farewell to Alan who drove off to deliver more aid. Soon our Air Croatia jet was rising into the clouds above that depressing city en route to Geneva and safety. For the first time, Simon and I compared thoughts about our experiences.

'I have a secret, Simon, which I have been itching to tell you,' I said.

'Strange,' he replied. 'So have I.'

'Well,' I told him, 'you recall that soldier we met on the first night in Lipik. He has threatened to shoot us both if I write anything he doesn't like about Marina. And I'm sure he's deadly serious.'

Simon shook his head and considered the prospect. Then he spoke: 'That's pretty worrying. But I've got an even worse tale. You know how we always wondered about Alan and how he was so passionate about his truck?

'Well he told me on that first night in the cafe that he would never let the Serbs take his truck. If they stopped him at a roadblock he was determined to go down fighting for it.'

'In fact, he warned me that he had wired the truck up with grenades and was prepared to pull the pins out.

'And,' Simon delayed his final point, looking me directly in the eyes, 'that means we have spent the last few days driving round in a war zone in a Toyota that was wired to explode at any moment.'

I sank into the seat and considered how fortunate that we had not been confronted or ambushed by a fighting patrol. I thought of my wife, June, and my two young children, safe at home, unlike the many women and children we had seen in devastated Croatia. I could not believe how lucky we all were. And how little we appreciated our privileges.

It was a feeling which would return to me many times over the next six years.

II

IT WAS COLD AND DARK BEHIND THE BLAST CURTAINS

Sarajevo – January 1994

It was cold and dark behind the blast curtains. A child was crying at one end of the hospital ward. And the Bosnian doctor, an old man smiling wanly behind thick spectacles, was telling the children's story in a matter-of-fact manner.

'Here is Bojana, who is eight and has five wounds in the bowel, right arm lacerations and open fractures,' he said, his right hand indicating a tiny figure, with dark eyes and a face which the joy and hope of childhood had deserted.

'She was playing in the street three days ago when a grenade landed and killed her girlfriend who was eleven years old.

'Next is Nijaz who is six and was hit by what you call dum-dum bullets with explosive tips. Their points are cut or hollowed out and they fragment on impact with the body. He was also playing in the street and has suffered shattered legs.'

The doctor's uncomfortable smile disappeared completely when we reached the third child on the ward. He turned away, lowered his voice and told the story of Kenan. He was ten and unlikely to live much longer. The doctor was frustrated that the boy's liver problem would normally be treatable. Now, in a city gripped by a modern version of medieval siege warfare, he had neither the drugs nor the equipment to save his life.

Impulsively, I reached into my camera bag and decided that Kenan would be the one. I pulled out Hector, the dog with the cheesy grin. He was one of my daughter Janna's favourite toys. She had offered him up along with some of her sweets and clothes 'for the children in Sarajevo.' I was convinced I had found the rightful recipient of Hector. I placed the bright yellow figure gently on the dark blue pillow alongside the pale round face.

16

Instantly, I began to appreciate that this was an empty gesture. There was no joy in black-haired Kenan's eyes. Nothing. As I took his picture in what had become a reflex action, I still half hoped for the same playful reaction I had seen from the other children. But no. Nothing. Just two motionless eyes, pursed lips and a face as white as the snow outside his covered window. And alongside this desperately sick child, Hector was grinning madly.

Suddenly I felt ashamed of my actions. Pathetic. Voyeuristic. I knew that the publication of pictures of tragic children like Kenan would add to the worldwide revulsion about what was happening in Sarajevo. So too did the doctor. But the depth of his plight and the shallowness of my gesture in handing over the dog, made me turn and leave after stopping briefly to thank the still-unsmiling doctor for his help and kindness.

In the dark hospital corridor, I hardly noticed the distant mortar blasts and gunfire outside. It had become background music. Always there, but subliminal, until it burst into the occasional crescendo of close-up violence.

Like a giant sausage machine, this city seemed to be churning out a daily quota of men, women and children whose destination was its overflowing cemeteries or the purgatory of its freezing, understaffed hospital wards. Constantly I wondered what I was doing there. And, selfishly, I wondered if I would survive....

More than a year had passed since my return from devastated Lipik. The Christmas Convoy appeal had been a major success. The original plan had been to send a small group of minibuses, loaded with aid, from Norwich to Reading, the headquarters of the national charity, Feed the Children. It had soon become clear that the reaction from donors was becoming overwhelming, far in excess of that low-key exercise.

For months I had worked with a small team managing the tidal wave of high quality food parcels, bedding and winter clothing that we had requested from *Eastern Daily Press* readers. We had reached virtual burnout trying to handle the warehousing, packing, loading, customs clearance and transportation of 240 tonnes of aid. Eventually, the final figures staggered us: more than 10,000 boxes of aid – worth a nominal Customs total of £300,000 – were packed into twelve juggernauts and driven to Croatia in an operation paid for by £21,000 in cash donations.

Despite it all though, the war in Bosnia was continuing relentlessly. In the spring of 1993, the Vance-Owen plan, aimed at stabilising the region, had flowered and withered like so many others. Ordinary people voiced their anger at the inaction of world leaders, who were more concerned with political repercussions than the enforcement of moral rectitude with decisive military action against the renegade Bosnian Serbs. Almost daily, I was receiving calls from complete strangers asking if we could do something more to help. Most people did not know specifically what they wanted done, just something, however small, however insignificant. The opportunity was certainly there. We still had more than £5,000 in donations in our charity account. I was determined to use it effectively.

It was then the plan first started to form. I had been nominated for a national award for the convoy operation. And much to my surprise and embarrassment, I picked up the title of Campaigning Journalist of the Year at one of those 'glittering ceremonies' in London, which journalists love to hate. It was embarrassing because the convoy had been very much a team effort, which I tried vainly to put across whenever possible. I harboured this awful impression of myself grabbing some form of glory from the suffering of the many and the hard work of a few. Nothing could have been further from reality. This was not about me. It was about all those generous readers who had helped. It was also about anger and frustration, not awards.

I was determined to go on and do more. My chance came through a friendship I had formed with Bill Ward, the Essex-born livewire who was managing the private Bupa Hospital, near Norwich. He had supported the Convoy scheme wholeheartedly, even donating the ambulance which we had driven to Lipik. He too was frustrated by the lack of action to stop the atrocities. Over a business lunch, we hatched a scheme to send a surgical team into Bosnia to perform operations that were not available there. He had access to the relevant skilled people. He was also in touch with the medical charity, Médécins Sans Frontieres, which had a long history of such work.

First contact with MSF in London established that a plastic surgery team was needed. The planning would be delicate and fraught with unforeseen difficulties. And the destination would be the besieged Bosnian capital Sarajevo.

Most people were aware of the city's suffering. The previous summer, we had seen the television pictures of the siege starting. Canon shells slicing through the walls of apartment blocks.... Women and children, their faces bandaged and bleeding, being carried to makeshift field stations ... the airport invaded by Serb tanks ... the politicians beating their fists on tables. The multi-ethnic city had now been divided by the war. Once Tito's showpiece, its quarter of a million inhabitants boasted a rich educational and cultural background which set them aside from the rural hinterland. Built along the Miljacka river valley, the city boasts rich Ottoman architecture, crowned by the Old Town, filled with wooden shops in cobbled streets. But there are also many stern Communist high rise monstrosities, as well as the sub-Wagnerian municipal buildings which display the decades of rule from Vienna by the Habsburgs.

Since the previous summer the Bosnian Serbs, backed by the artillery of the Serb-controlled Yugoslav National Army, the JNA, had taken over several districts and moved into the ring of hills which gave a command-ing view of almost every street in the city. From there, they had rained a murderous hail of fire onto the civilians and the flimsy defending forces of the Bosnian Army. Thousands had been killed or maimed by the indis-criminate sniping and shelling.

It was with some trepidation that I worked throughout the second half of 1993 on the details of our mission to Sarajevo. I had seen the genocide of the Serbs in Croatia the previous year. But it was not even close to the scale of the Bosnian capital. It was difficult to comprehend how the surgi-cal team was going to fly in and out of an airport and city under fire and conduct operations for two weeks. But I had underestimated the experi-ence of MSF. The mission, which we called Operation Sarajevo, was to come under the medical charity's complete control. That included the signing of contracts by each team member to ensure they abided by their strict security code. It also included the wearing of flak jackets and hel-mets at all times outside, checking in regularly on mobile radios, and using only armoured vehicles. Any non-compliance would mean a team member could be sent home immediately by the security chief. At meet-ings with MSF staff in London and Amsterdam, we were told: 'We have never lost a medical volunteer on any mission anywhere in the world – and we don't intend to start now.'

Despite such precautions, Sarajevo had moved that year into the top three of the world's most dangerous places. I wondered what the other two were. Consequently, membership of the five-strong team, all based in Norwich, would have to be purely voluntary. Our first full meeting took place at Bill's Bupa Hospital, where I was introduced and the guidelines were established. I had already agreed with MSF to sign up as one of the charity's logisticians, to avoid any problems passing through military defence lines as a journalist.

The team elected as leader the consultant anaesthetist, Ken MacIntosh, a middle-aged Midlander with useful experience as a colonel in the Terri-torial Army. The lead surgeon was Allan Bardsley, a consultant in plastic and reconstructive work, whose ascerbic Manchester wit would prove a godsend. The second plastic surgeon was Per Hall, a youthful, six-foot-four senior registrar. Another Mancunian with a strong line in demolition humour, Mandy O'Toole, theatre manager at the Bupa hospital, was to act as theatre nurse on the mission.

From the start, it was clear that Ken, so used to command in his part-time military duties, would prove formidable in the team leader role. After some months of delicate negotiations to reach this position, I found myself having to provide him with reassurance that I was not 'a wet-behind the ears junior reporter, but an experienced senior journalist who could handle all the sensitive medical and military confidentiality we would encounter.' That established, mutual respect quickly grew in our subsequent meetings.

We all knew we were going into the unknown and there was a chance that some might not return. All of us had loved-ones who were nervous of our involvement in the mission. Between them, Allan and Per had five small children, who, like mine, were having difficulty coming to terms with the reason their fathers had volunteered to travel to a city which was shown under bombardment almost every evening on the television news.

Agonisingly, the mission was held up through the winter. At one point, it seemed the Serbs were about to launch a full-scale assault on Sarajevo. It was difficult to understand how such an apparently well-equipped military machine was being held back by defenders armed largely with home-made weapons and whatever they could smuggle through a supposedly secret tunnel under the airport. Since the siege had begun in May 1992, there had been countless pitched battles followed by a truce, which was broken daily. The death toll from the Bosnian Public Health Institute recorded 9,338 war casualties in the city in 16 months. Of those, 1,505 were children. In the most recent report, covering the final week of September, 1993, 11 civilians were killed and 59 wounded. Indeed, this was a dangerous city.

Christmas came with mixed blessings for most of us. But sponsorship had rolled in from numerous companies throughout the UK. We even had a complete set of Arctic clothing, put together under Ken's military direction. It included silk vests and long johns, heavy boots, gloves and liners and waterproof jackets and liners – all in blue to identify us instantly (a point which was later to disturb me continually in those sniper-ridden streets). Thick down sleeping bags, Swiss Army knives and water bottles were among the mass of kit selected to help us face the war zone and its temperatures which could fall to minus 20 Centigrade.

In the forefront of it all was Bill Ward, who had also wanted to make the trip, but was told by MSF that they could not justify his inclusion without the relevant skills. Disappointed, the perpetually active hospital manager continued to apply his managerial ability to planning. He would also become a near-manically efficient home base contact during the team's mission. Like all of us, he knew that people were dying each week on Sarajevo's streets and every detail had to be covered. Among the precautions taken was a full medical check and inoculations for the whole team. MSF had warned that the only immunisation required was for hepatitis A. But being physicians, no chances were taken. Sarajevo had had interruptions to its water and electricity supplies for over a year, its food was either emergency aid or of uncertain origin and its drug supplies were low. As a result, we all felt like pin cushions after Bill's vaccination programme was completed.

After Christmas, meetings with MSF in London and Amsterdam resulted in a mid-January departure deadline.

We began to bond as a team. The stress-relieving Mancunian humour of Allan and Mandy would prove to be an uplifting asset throughout the horrors to come. Per was quieter. Ken maintained an air of inner strength and military bearing. I wondered what they made of me, the journalist who had been as unhinged as them in getting involved in this exercise into the unknown.

When departure day arrived, it was the middle of January and we were all pretty tense. Money had poured in from *Eastern Daily Press* readers – almost £60,000, more than three times what we had estimated – and there had been continuing media coverage of the slaughter in Bosnia, including the murder of a British lorry driver delivering aid near Zenica. There was an air of unreality at the airport as interviews were conducted for what was dubbed 'Britain's first mercy team heading for hell city'. In the comfortable front lounge, I felt unease at the hugs and kisses among the team and their loved ones. Some of the children were old enough to understand their fathers were going somewhere unusual. The publicity was so intense that we had to give them our own version of the facts. My own children, Janna and Jared, were aware that there was a possibility I might not be coming home. It was an oppressive thought which was to cause them some mental trauma over the days ahead. June and I maintained our tradition of 'not appearing too worried' whenever such moments emerged. Behind the front, though, we admitted later to each other that we both harboured grave doubts about the trip.

The next two days did nothing to dispel those fears. After changing planes in Amsterdam we were soon bumping down on the runway at the same damp and depressing Zagreb I had seen before. The Intercontinental Hotel had not changed. In the foyer was the same collection of blue berets sported by snappily-uniformed officers from a variety of countries, as well as sharp-suited arms dealers who hover around war zones like vultures. There were also a few of those adventure seekers in bright waterproof jackets who became a familiar sight in Bosnia. One of them, a Frenchman, once told me he had taken his camcorder to the Afghan war and asked me for a lift, adding with an odd smile: 'But only if you are going to the front line.'

They are the kind of people who cause you to check your own motives for being there. In my case, I had come out of frustration and anger at the inaction of politicians to stop the slaughter. I had seen the horrors of the Croatian war already and was too frightened of dying to have any sense of adventure on my agenda. Yes, there was curiosity, a need to experience closeness with people who were suffering, a desire to do what little we could to help. I knew the team felt the same. In Ken's case, as a part-time soldier, there was also the professional interest in coping under fire. But all of them held that physician's desire to apply their skills in such an unfamiliar environment. Perhaps they could save lives and limbs. Certainly they would learn a great deal about war surgery.

Over the next two days in Zagreb, we were kept on standby. The airlift into Sarajevo was always uncertain. The UN had christened it 'Maybe Airlines' and had even drawn up documents and stickers marked accordingly. One Italian transport plane had been shot down and many had been hit by small arms fire in the past year. The airport was under UN control as a humanitarian aid lifeline for the encircled city. But the Serbs regularly caused a halt through renegade units firing sporadically or through organised sniping of aircraft. As a result we did not know how we would get into the city. We were told it might mean a straightforward United Nations Protection Force (UNPROFOR) flight from Zagreb, south to skirt the beautiful Croatian Adriatic coastline, turning inland over the once-popular resort of Split and diving steeply at Kiseljak to avoid ground fire on the approach to Sarajevo.

Alternatively, and more worryingly, we might have to fly directly to Split and take a UN helicopter to Kiseljak. From there we would make a difficult overland trip by armoured vehicle through the front lines and into Sarajevo. Both prospects were daunting and occupied our minds.

As a result, we passed the time in periods tinged, in equal measure, by sublime tranquillity and increasing foreboding. We swam in the hotel pool, shared its sauna with overweight German and Croatian businessmen and had a whip-round for a meal to celebrate Allan's forty-first birthday in the well-appointed restaurant. In between were MSF's regular briefings about the threats we were to face.

Dana Van Alphen, a trained doctor and the charity's Zagreb co-ordinator, spelled it out: 'What you have seen on TV is nothing like the reality. It will shock you. The sheer enormity of the destruction is hard to take in. It is like Dresden would appear to you.

'After you arrive at the airport you will be taken in our armoured vehicle very fast along sniper alley. You will see how the city has turned into a living hell. The destruction is so extensive it will be depressing for you.

'But we will keep you safe in our houses and you will move to and from

22

the hospital only in armoured vehicles. Our two houses are among the few in the street with windows that have not been blown out. The main problem is a sniper who moved in three weeks ago and shoots regularly down the street. In the dark, we must insist, no torches must be used.

'Very soon, I can assure you, you will be recognising and counting the incoming and outgoing rounds. No problem.'

With that, the Dutch woman leaned back, smiled grimly, and sucked hard on another of the Marlboroughs which she appeared to be chain-smoking. It was a habit we would find was universal in 'hell city'.

MSF proved exceptionally thorough. We were taken through the layout of the city and the front lines. We were given our security rules and the warning that any breach would mean the ignominy of being sent home like an errant schoolchild. And we were fitted with our bulletproof helmets, marked with our names and blood groups, 'to be worn outside and whilst travelling at all times'. There were also our special bullet proof jackets. These were high quality lifesavers, made from the best armoured plating around, tough, lightweight Kevlar, they also boasted a ceramic insert over the heart. Many deaths from high velocity weapons, we were told, are caused by the massive kinetic energy delivered by the round. Stopping a bullet dead could still mean your vital organs would collapse from the huge shockwave that resulted. The ceramic plate would absorb a proportion of that shockwave and provide additional stopping cover over one of the sniper's favourite targets, your chest area. Another useful asset would be our UN blue cards. We would keep these attached to our necks constantly, like talismen, as our last hope of survival if the city was overrun. In any major assault by the Serbs, the UN was committed to evacuating all staff wearing the blue card. Without it, you were lost. In what was known as a 'Condition Black' situation, in which the assault would have been too quick and intensive for the UN to respond, the advice was 'do everything you are told and pray'.

In case any of us felt that this was a siege involving an unsophisticated bunch of lunatics, firing wildly in an alcoholic haze, we were also put right. Yes, there were Chetniks in the mountains around Sarajevo. These were the irregulars, like Arkan's Tigers, who had butchered and raped their way through Croatia and Bosnia, without apparent military discipline or any cognizance of the Geneva Convention. But even they had been working to political direction from Belgrade. We would become familiar with the 'Slivovic Unload', that time of the evening when some of the oppressors would launch into a round of heavy firing under the influence of their strong national spirit. And yes, the mornings would be quieter because they would be suffering hangovers. But, generally, the siege was being conducted with studious precision by a force which had inherited much of the hardware of the well-equipped Yugoslav National Army. That included artillery, heavy and light mortars and highly accurate sniping weapons. A favourite was the Simonov. Another was the Dragunov, a standard sniper rifle among Russian special forces and capable of hitting a man-sized target easily at 600 metres. At Sarajevo Airport, we were told, certain snipers specialised in maiming the French Foreign Legion UN troops currently in control. A number had been evacuated with bullet wounds in the hand caused by single shots from snipers up to 800 metres away. Overlooking the deadliest stretch of road into the city, known as Sniper Alley, was a trench filled by a group of mercenaries, known to some as The Hunters. These were known to include crackshot European and American soldiers of fortune who had poured fire onto men, women and children since the siege began. It had been reported that they sometimes offered a days' shooting, at a price, to professional hunters keen to pick off some unique quarry ... human beings.

When we were whisked off finally on the Monday to Zagreb military airport, we were all far better equipped mentally to face Sarajevo. Almost routinely we walked out in milky sunshine to the huge, white Illyushin jet transport. We were sharing the UN-chartered monster with its Russian crew, a collection of returning 'blue berets' and media people who were foolhardy enough to make the trip. It seemed almost any non-Bosnian with a plausible reason could apply successfully for a blue card and a seat on what must have been the world's most dubious airline at that time. Ironically, I later discovered that rich Bosnians were offering up to $5000 US for a blue card to take them to safety.

The flight was cold and noisy as we pretended to read novels, sitting in the jump seats that lined the sides of the interior of the aircraft's belly. Most of the space was taken up with tonnes of huge tins of soup, held in place by netting. As I stared at this monstrous wall of metal, I wondered if the straps would prevent it from lurching towards me, flattening me against the wall during some emergency manoeuvre. I could imagine the headline: 'Mercy crew crushed in Sarajevo soup tragedy'. It didn't bear further consideration.

I need not have worried. The approach to the city was straight out of the Russian special forces textbook.

After Kiseljak, we turned east and dived through the clouds to power in just over the red roofs of countless abandoned farms and villages. Through a tiny window I marvelled at the haunting beauty of the snow-covered land which was rushing by at such speed. It was early on a sun-kissed afternoon when the wheels touched down and the huge beast came quickly to a stop.

The tension was palpable as we heaved our rucksacks down the aircraft ladder in full view of the sniper-infested hills. The process seemed to take forever, as we stood in the bright sunshine fully aware that we were now in the sights of anyone who chose to shoot at the foreign figures in the blue Gore-tex jackets. We also knew that the 80-metre run from the jet to the aircraft buildings would be some of the most dangerous few seconds of the whole mission.

'If you can see hills in Sarajevo, then the snipers can see you too,' we had been told by MSF. And we could see hills all around us on that wide open runway.

The French Legionnaire flightmaster pointed to the safety area and told us to move quickly as we started our separate runs. Under the weight of the baggage, helmet and flak jacket, I struggled to keep my feet on the icy tarmac. All the time, out in the open, breathing heavily, I could feel that tingling on the back of my neck (a sensation that was to become commonplace) as I considered the crosshairs of a sniperscope being levelled at that point between my helmet and my collar. Finally, behind the sandbagged barrier, I joined Mandy and tried to regain some dignity. She told me later how worried she had been: 'I was really frightened. You get a sense of panic and space that you don't normally take notice of. It felt very much a case that "the hills have eyes". It was just important to me to get somewhere under cover. The noise from the aircraft must have been tremendous, but I didn't hear a thing, not a thing.'

Behind steel containers, we were greeted by the smiling faces of our hosts from MSF and taken in two armoured, former bank security trucks through the front lines into the city. It was a curious reality that the drive took us through checkpoints operated by both sides, who were just a short no-man's land apart.

Behind the thick, bulletproof windows, a desperate world unfolded before our eyes. First would come the Serb strongpoint where the troops in their green and purple camouflaged uniforms would check papers and then radio ahead to their Bosnian enemies that we had been cleared to head through. Later, I discovered that these soldiers had been at school together and would have regular radio exchanges about old times and the wellbeing of their respective friends from either side of the current divide.

The gap between the lines was a zone of utter devastation. Hardly a wall or a fence was standing, as if the area had been carpet-bombed. Here and there were burned out vehicles, including two heavy tanks with their tracks blown off, their guns drooping downward. Rags and footwear were sticking out of the snow. Everywhere were the remains of previous life: roofless, windowless villas, twisted rails, fire-blackened shops. Truly a Dresden, bereft of life save for the few brave souls who were clinging on in this zone of hell.

Once through the Bosnian Army's striped barrier, we were skirting Dobrinja, the apartment suburb built for the Winter Olympics in which the British ice dance duo Jane Torvill and Christopher Dean had scored their near-legendary perfect 6s. They would hardly recognise the place now. A few people were running between the housing blocks. But at the end of each road were tall steel barriers, burned-out vehicles and sandbags, protection against the snipers who overlooked the whole area.

On a nearby slope, desperate locals had dared to create vegetable plots, but they stopped halfway up. Any higher, I was told, and they would have been swept by sniper fire. Many a Sarejevan had already died trying to produce a cabbage or a lettuce for his malnourished children. We had already seen the ironic graffiti on two walls. The first said simply: 'Welcome to Hell'. The next, more subtly, said: 'Tito, come back, all is forgiven'. Below it, in a copy of the dead Yugoslav leader's Cyrillic script, someone had added: 'You must be bloody joking!'

As we swung right at Halilovici, crossing the red Miljacka river, we were soon heading down Sniper Alley, that landmark so familiar to viewers of Independent Television News and the BBC. It is here that the Serbs had occupied and fortified districts on the south bank of the river and had their clearest view of Bosnians moving along the main road on the north side. Hundreds had died from the shelling and sniping that had swept the road from those trenches and the high rise apartment blocks of the far bank.

As our driver speeded up the heavy truck, we were overtaken by an old green VW Golf, without windows. Its driver flashed past at more than 120 kilometres an hour, clearly anxious not to present a good target.

But this was a 'quiet' day, we were told. Many people had been brought out by the lull, especially in the main central streets of Novo Sarajevo, where we passed pedestrians hauling water containers and piles of wood on makeshift trolleys.

'More people die on quiet days, however,' said our MSF security chief, Freek Landmeter, a former Dutch construction expert in his twenties. 'It seems quiet. People come out of hiding, then pouff, a shell comes in from nowhere and catches a lot of people out on the streets at once.'

No sooner were we swinging into the MSF office car park at the Kosevo Hospital than the crumps of shelling could be heard in the distance, followed by the rattle of machine guns. On a floor above the office I noticed part of a wall was missing and hospital beds were protruding. Later, I learned, that was where a group of recuperating patients had been recently killed or maimed by a mortar shell. Even hospitals, it appeared, were not immune to this killing machine. Inside the office the composed Freek oozed authority and confidence as he provided a detailed update on the security position. Next we were introduced to Dr Anadi Begic, the young plastic surgeon who was the only remaining member of the dozen who once ran the Kosovo's reconstructive surgery unit. The others had left, some escaping to safety overseas with their families through the 'secret' tunnel under the airport. Anadi was under huge strain, attempting to hold together an eighteen-bed department with a huge demand for surgery and a wide variety of patients. White faced and hollow-eyed, he talked in clear English about the workload. Much was already known to the team from MSF reports. High and low velocity gunshot wounds had torn through the bodies of military and civilian patients, causing complex and potentially crippling, if not fatal, damage. Some had been hit eighteen months earlier, further reducing their chances of recovery. Others had been badly burned in apartment blasts caused by do-it-yourself attempts to rig up their homes with garden hoses to the city's gas heating supplies.

We toured a few beds in the unheated wards, their stark decor illuminated by the snow laden sky which was visible through windows mostly covered in hole-splattered UNHCR polythene sheeting. The faces were those of old men and women, civilians with crippling injuries; as well as gaunt young men who had seen the horrors of the front line, their bodies emaciated by malnutrition and the atrophy which comes after a long period of hopelessness. One man had lain in bed for so long that his bed sores had opened a wound which covered much of his right thigh and buttock. I had never seen such a huge crater in a living human body, with his thigh bone and musculature fully exposed.

The team maintained a calm professional interest as Anadi talked though a selection of cases and passed Allan and Per their notes. I have to admit to being fascinated by the prospect of their skills bringing respite for some of these people. I had only witnessed an operation once before. That was for a three-part newspaper feature on a cancer sufferer. I never wrote the final part. He died soon after leaving surgery. Fortunately, I am one of those people who is amazed, rather than repulsed, by the complex workings of the human body. Those Catholic nuns had also instilled in me their philosophy of the sacred gift which life represents and the boundless potential which death, too, can bring.

The team must have sensed this. For soon afterwards, on our way to our accommodation in the armoured bank truck, Per asked if I would be happy to operate his special macro-lens close-up camera with a ring flash for taking educational slides of the operations they would perform.

'Why not?' I replied, 'at least I might be useful doing that rather than getting in the way.' Mandy and Allan laughed. But I wondered if they thought I would be up to it over the coming days. I wondered too.

It was getting dark when we arrived at the house. Freek jumped out of the truck first and dashed to open the front door, signalling for us to follow quickly. With our baggage bouncing off each other we crunched through the snow. A few explosions and distant gunfire could be heard. We were aware of the warning in Zagreb about our 'friendly neighbourhood sniper' who might be up there, waiting for just such an exotic new target. We all made it safely.

The house was surprisingly comfortable. It was in the middle of a street of suburban villas, on a slope overlooking the city. Across the road was a second villa, which Allan and Per would use for sleeping. Inside, the main house was freezing, apart from the living room, which was lit by a huge Naptha stove. It felt like a sunburst after the below zero conditions of the hospital. This room was to bring us respite every evening from the horrors of the day. MSF knew the value of warmth as a psychological boost for the foreign teams who had passed through before us. In the basement we found evidence of their presence: boxes of combat rations from several UN member armies. These, too, would provide a great lift over the coming nights, as the basis of the wonderful meals which the team would concoct. Such delights as Dutch army stroganoff and Italian pasta casserole, washed down with French army red wine would make us feel a little guilty as well as like millionaires in a city of paupers.

Upstairs, the house was teeth-jarringly cold. With just a few unpredictable hours of electricity a day, we were to become well used to candles and torchlight. In the gloom I parked my bags in the first room, which was twin bedded. Ken took the other bed. That left Mandy to her own room nearby. And Freek had his room at the end of the corridor.

That night we ate a welcome hot meal, reviewed our activities and planned for the operations that had been identified for the day ahead. After a large glass of the duty-free Glenmorangie malt which we had been advised would be vital to the mission, we turned in. The unlit and unheated bathroom proved a struggle, particularly as the near-icy water came from buckets and drums collected by MSF. It is too easy to ignore basic hygiene in such circumstances. But in an unspoken pact, we were all conscious that our appearance and actions would be studied closely by everyone we met. We had to maintain our dignity and morale out of respect for the people we were attempting to help. And, after all, someone had risked their life to fetch the water from a collection point so it would have been desperately ungrateful not to have used it.

I was also grateful for the silk vest and longjohns which Ken had recommended as vital cold-busters. I had worn them all day under the thick wool shirt, pullover, fleece and Gore-tex jacket, windproof trousers, thick walking socks and heavy leather boots. Now I would be wearing them to bed in the all-weather, duck-down sleeping bag which I zipped myself into, exhausted and ready for a deep, deep slumber. Yet, despite the fatigue and the Glenmorangie, sleep failed to come. Ken was dictating his diary into a Walkman on the next bed. But my head was spinning. And I was worrying. The house, we had been told, was so close to the Serb lines that it would be unlikely to be hit – which seemed like one of those ironic Bosnian jokes. If it were hit, there would be no warning, just the blast first followed by the slower speed sound of the mortar bomb or artillery shell arriving. In any war zone, it is familiar to see people flinching or ducking at the sound of a nearby blast or bullet. Generally it is too late. Most of the metal flying around is travelling faster than sound. So, when you hear it, you have already been hit. Or you have been lucky.

Even so, I spent what seemed like hours that first night, listening to the ripples of automatic gunfire and watching the occasional flicker of the explosions which came every few minutes, penetrating the shadows of the large protective wall that stood opposite our rear-facing window.

Daylight brought another snowy scene and a steaming mug of tea from Ken, who was up before any of us. Breakfast was an odd selection of army ration biscuits, cheeses and jam, with lots of good French coffee. Mandy had slept surprisingly well and Freek was already kitted out for the day, organis-ing the armoured truck on his personal radio. His air of dependable author-ity was a constant source of comfort for all of us, and there was no doubt that if we broke his rules, he would have us on the next mercy lift out.

By the time I had staggered along the corridor and opened the front door, Ken was already outside, crouching in the snow, his helmet buckled and the thick garden wall sheltering him from the sniper in the hill at the top end of the street. Military efficiency, I thought. Then I considered the depth of my own ignorance of such matters. I was like a lamb in a slaugh-terhouse. But I was hoping to escape the butcher's block.

At the hospital, the real business of our mission began. During that first day, the team carried out three delicate operations in very basic condi-tions. Using microsurgery techniques, they gave hope to two young men who had lost the use of hands after being hit, separately, by a heavy machine-gun and a low velocity bullet, probably from a pistol. One case was skin grafting for an old woman whose face and body had been badly burned by a gas explosion. I used the close-up camera throughout, hoping I was being useful in providing useable slides for war surgery lectures back home. The grafting had been fascinating. The team had taken layers of skin from sections of the old woman's body and placed them on her seri-ously burned face and upper body. To a layman, the removal of the skin had resembled a fine cheese-grating procedure. It left a painful spot, which would heal in time. And it was preferable to the excruciating pain and dis-figurement of the burnt tissue.

Through it all, the unit's remaining staff and doctors remained curious, polite and friendly. They had worked with the country's finest surgeons before the siege. Now, nineteen months later, they were assisting foreigners in that work. They had boasted well-equipped operating theatres and advanced techniques. Now most of their doctors had gone. The drugs and the machines had become unreliable. And without proper power, water and hygienic supplies, those left were struggling to cope.

Many of their colleagues had been killed on the way to and from the hospital. In a city where twenty Marlborough cigarettes cost five Deutschmarks (£2) and a one-pound jar of coffee could fetch 100 DM (£40), the nurses were working for army pay of just 1.5 DM (60 pence) a month.

One young nurse told me how she would virtually live all week in the hospital: 'At least here we have food, beans and biscuits, some warmth and beds. There is also some security. Two of my friends who were killed on the walk home would not stay here because they had families and wanted to be home with them. It cost them their lives.

'How can you judge what is the best? Now, after so many have died and so many have escaped, single people like me want to escape, before we die too. We thought at first we should stay and do our best. But this has gone on so long and there seems no end, only cruelty and death. You are the only people now helping. For that we thank you, but it is not enough to make us stay. There has been too much misery.'

Like many she did not want to be named. There was an air of fear everywhere about speaking out. This was uncharacteristic of the Sarajevan people. Like free-spirited Amsterdam, they had a tradition of radicalism and free speech, a superior cosmopolitanism which set them apart from the provincialism of Tito's largely rural conglomeration of ethnic groupings. 'I am Sarajevan first and Bosnian second,' the young nurse told me, echoing a common sentiment. Like many in the city, she was not even born a Bosnian Muslim, but a Croat originally. In the national census, Sarajevo had the highest percentage of people who had called themselves, simply, Yugoslavs.

During the siege, British television and Press reports labelled them Muslims. But only a small proportion of them actually practised the faith. And the Bosnian army had Serbs and Croats as well as Bosnians fighting for Sarajevo at all levels. Such surprises and contradictions were everywhere.

On a walk between hospital units, Mandy and I came across a group of nurses whom I photographed. All were elegantly dressed in fur or fashionably cut long coats, their hair and face make-up in perfect order. Mandy was fascinated at how they had managed.

'Dignity,' replied a blonde nurse, her lips bright red with gloss. 'If we have to stay, then we will stay with dignity, not as slaves. Everyone finds a little something from somewhere. We have survived. Our clothes are either home-made or we have re-cut them from aid handouts.'

Another nurse agreed. She smiled as she told us: 'We say in Sarajevo that we are women still and if we must die then we will die and be beautiful corpses, not ugly beggars. That is our wish.'

It was on one such walk in the grounds that we came across one woman who had not survived so well. It was snowing quite hard and was well below freezing when we saw her. She was dressed in a light cardigan, carrying her baby daughter. Mandy had wanted to find a deserving child for her special teddy bear. This was that child. We walked up with our interpreter and Mandy asked if she could hand over the bear.

The gaunt and anxious woman smiled when she realised what we were offering. 'Of course,' said our interpreter, 'She says for her daughter Irma this will be her first toy. Her home was destroyed when she was in hospital having Irma and she had to live in the hospital for months afterward. But life now is very hard.'

'She has had to leave hospital to allow patients to use the bed.'

Asked where the father was, the interpreter shrugged at the woman's reply. Missing, dead or captured, the woman did not say, only thanked us and walked into the snow. Mandy was visibly moved: 'We gave her a little teddy and she thought we had given her the world.'

An hour later, with sniping and shelling increasing, we were on our way back up the hill in the armoured truck when we spotted someone familiar in the still-falling snow. It was Irma and her mother. She had been carrying the child who was still clutching the bear. Both were soaked from the snow and facing the potential of death from a mortar at any moment.

We did not stop. There were thousands like little Irma in Sarajevo. All I could do was tell her story when I sent my article that night via the satellite fax at the MSF office. It was our only link with the outside world and I didn't even know if the words were getting through. I could only hope that by helping to shed a light on the cruel reality of the siege, some politicians might be forced to act decisively. I was wrong.

Next day, at the hospital I noticed from the window that there were more black marks in the snow on the soccer pitch below. I counted eleven. Yesterday there had been four. These were the graves of those who had died overnight or been killed in the latest shelling and sniping. With round-the-clock sniping and an average of 260 explosions a day in a city of around 380,000, including refugees, a statistician would have an easy time working out his survival chances.

Mandy and I made a visit to see more of the young victims. I could not help conclude that the Serbs in the surrounding hills were little more than genocidal maniacs when the children's stories emerged. We saw a dozen, most with shrapnel or bullet wounds picked up on the playgrounds or streets in recent weeks. Some were also badly burned. And, on top of their injuries, some had been orphaned in the blasts which they had survived.

Upstairs we joined Allan, Per and Ken for an operation on an old woman whose apartment had been blasted by a mortar. A piece of shrapnel had gouged a huge trough in the top of her head and the surgeons opted for a skull flap to fill the indentation.

That afternoon, Freek took me to the UN headquarters for a presentation by MSF of its psychological survey of the city. The concrete and steel building was a favourite target of the Serbs. As we passed through the French Foreign Legion checkpoints, cannon fire began to hit the perimeter area, kicking up clouds of smoke and dust. Inside, the tax free shop area, which sold such delights as 'UN Welcome to Sarajevo' teeshirts, was being repaired after an overnight shell had blown in part of the roof.

Four more shells rocked the fortress-like building during the hour-long meeting, but the dozens of delegates and media people present seemed little concerned. They heard a litany of tragedy from MSF's team. No fewer than seven out of ten deaths in the city were now caused by bullets or shelling. No wonder MSF's survey had found that almost one in ten of all households had someone suffering psychiatric problems requiring professional help.

Understandably, after seventy-six weeks of hell, some people were going out of their minds.

After just two days, I could understand their pain a little better. Just the simplest activity could spell death. Running out of wood, food or water meant a walk along streets where death was coming without warning to as few as three people on the quiet days and to scores when the Serbs turned up the heat. On trips in the truck down sniper alley, I was aware of the occasional bullet hissing past. Milan, our young Bosnian driver, simply grumbled at the inconvenience. I knew we were relatively safe behind steel that had been tested with a burst of Kalashnikov fire from close range. But what of those countless people on the streets?

As Nadja, a Kosevo hospital nurse, told me: 'Life is hell. That is the plain truth. It is also, as you say, like Russian roulette, but we must play the game. You can die from starvation or from thirst or from cold. Instead you can die from a bullet or grenade. The choice is yours and you live with it each day, day after day.'

The only delights were the occasional treats from aid workers like us. Our chocolate, coffee and sweets were prized by the nurses. Indeed, one desperate young woman made clear that for a packet of sought-after

Marlborough, a key currency, she would be happy to share an intimate tryst in a quiet side room. Her offer was declined, but symbolised the desperation of these people.

One delight Sarajevo would not miss was music. And it was to the Gallerija Obala that Mandy and I went with Freek for one of the most moving performances I have ever witnessed. Inside were a couple of hundred Sarajevans and foreigners who had gathered for a photographic slide show by British cameraman Paul Lowe.

The atmosphere was that of an arts centre in England, apart from the explosions in the streets outside. Everyone there knew the event had been well publicised and would have been considered by the Serbs as a possible atrocity target. A well-aimed howitzer or heavy mortar shot would have been devastating.

Even so, people had come in defiance and to uphold the city's cultural tradition that had seen a cinema, theatre and music centre continue to operate through the siege. As the lights went down the pictures filled the screen, scenes of the city's suffering, and the lamenting strains of the Adaggio from the Sarajevo String Quartet drifted up from the corner of the room. It was a stark and moving experience that drew a line of defiance in the sand.

As the week wore on, the team's successes mounted. Operations were running into double figures, scores of outpatients had been assessed and they had also conducted some training and education sessions which had been a major morale boost to Anadi and his team. I had compiled a huge stock of photographs and filed copy on the satfax every evening. The message was certainly getting out and the shelling had reduced.

I still had some chocolate in my holdall and decided I would hand it out to children near the hospital. I was breaking Freek's rules, but the unit had become claustrophobic. As a journalist I still felt I had not touched the heart of this city and never really would.

After a short walk round the main block I came to a sector overlooking the Olympic ice stadium, now partially collapsed under the heavy bombardment of the Serbs. There was the usual sporadic shooting in progress in the distance. I passed out the chocolate to a boy and girl who were walking by along a footpath which was regularly swept by snipers. Instead of saving it they wolfed it down immediately, smiling broadly, then made their way to the snowy slopes nearby. I pulled out my camera and began taking pictures of the children and the stadium when the first shots came in.

Two, followed by another, seconds later. The third thumped, hammer hard, into a concrete wall alongside me and threw some dust into my eyes. Only then did it dawn on me. I was being fired at.

I dived behind the wall, shaking, still rubbing my eyes. I did not have a clue where the rounds had come from or if I would be safe to leave. Instead, I crouched there for at least twenty-five minutes. Mist was descending with the gathering gloom which, I knew, would make the sniper's task more difficult. I knew I had to get back or Freek would be seeking me out, with potentially embarrassing consequences. So I tightened my bag strap, zipped up my blue coat, took a deep breath and ran the half mile back to the plastics unit. I decided not to mention the incident. I had gone out for some air and it had been a mistake. My mistake. And almost a very costly one.

Next day my week was up and I was due to fly out, leaving the surgical team to continue for another week. My feelings of guilt were gut-wrenching. I had to return to work in Norwich, but hoped that Maybe Airlines were failing to operate.

To my chagrin, a morning flight was scheduled. I was feeling awful, like a deserter, when the truck pulled up at the safe house that night and Mandy and I stepped out. Then, as we headed for the door, a close burst of heavy machine gun fire split through the dark street. I grabbed her and pushed her to the floor, receiving a faceful of snow for my trouble. As the firing continued, I looked up to see our Dutch security man sliding a key into the lock.

'Freek, get down, that's close, that must be our local sniper,' I shouted.

He stepped inside, looked down at the two sprawled figures, shrugged and replied: 'No, it is not him James. Don't worry, it is outgoing fire.'

We drank more of the Glenmorangie that night and smoked some Marlboroughs. Even though none of us really smoked normally, it seemed like a palliative for the stress and tension. I packed my bags and took messages to loved-ones with the promise that I would see the team the following week at Norwich Airport.

Next morning I felt even more down about leaving. I was still praying for an aborted flight when I shook hands with Freek at Sarajevo International Airport, ran to the Illyushin and strapped myself in for the take-off.

It was a long and worrying week before the team came home. Bill, in his ebullient style, went out to Amsterdam to join them on their stopover for a celebratory dinner. I waited for them to arrive at Norwich Airport the next day. We all spoke at the media reception which followed.

There was no doubt they had saved lives. More than thirty operations had been conducted by the 'fun team' as they had been labelled. They had sung rugby songs when the electricity had failed midway through a delicate surgical procedure. They had joked their way through rocket and mortar blasts. They had saved limbs, restored the use of hands, repaired horribly disfigured faces and bodies. And they had shown that people in Britain cared.

That is really what it was all about.

III

THEN THE SERBS CAME

Operation Mostar – March 1994

Little Admir Vele loved to play football.

His home was a village in the steep hills above Mostar, the historic city which sits astride the blue-green waters of the Neretva river.

Then the Serbs came.

At the age of seven, Admir was burned out of his house and was unlikely to play any sport again. He hobbled painfully with the aid of a wooden crutch after his right leg had been shattered by a shotgun blast.

He was lucky. Many of his friends died in the onslaught which had become increasingly brutal and had turned the one-time tourist trap into a charnel house. The city's struggle was as bewilderingly complex as any. It had been one of Bosnia's most beautiful gems, with its ancient Turkish marketplace and buildings, nestling in a deep valley. Its four-centuries-old arched bridge had survived thirty earth tremors and had graced a million postcards before it was finally blasted into the river in November, 1993.

The seeds of unrest had been sown in the 1950s when Croats from the belligerent, adjoining Hercegovinia outback moved in, bringing their insular rural views to a city where a Bosnian majority had integrated for so long with their Serb neighbours and friends. However, the city's military airport and strategic position identified it as a major prize for the rampaging Serbs when the Bosnian war began in April, 1992. They surrounded Mostar and began its systematic destruction. Many thousands of Bosnians joined the Croat HVO forces in the hope that they would have sufficient combined strength to beat off their attackers. But when their efforts failed, the Croats turned on the Bosnians, herding 55,000 of them into a ghetto on the city's east bank. It was a classic case of ethnic cleansing. An indescribable hail of shells, mortar bombs and bullets rained down on the enclave. Serbs in the surrounding hills and Croats on the west bank both

35

sought to annihilate their one-time Muslim friends and neighbours with a curtain of sustained fire. Conditions had been worse than in Sarajevo. Worse even than in Vukovar, the Croat town levelled by the Serbs and often paraded as the ultimate icon of the worst effects of ethnic cleansing.

At least in Vukovar the Croatian army had managed to bring in regular supplies of ammunition and food to the defenders. The Bosnian Muslims of Mostar lived like rats trapped in cellars. Without the benefit of air power, their oppressors had managed to replicate the effects of carpet bombing using artillery.

Countless people died from thirst, starvation, disease and the hail of high explosive, emerging from the darkness during quiet periods to create yet more of the graves which can be seen on every green space.

Yet Admir had survived. With his little brother Adnan, aged three, and his strict and resourceful mother Senada, twenty-eight, a one-time textile factory worker, he had resisted a child's temptation to stray. Their father Muhamed, thirty-two, had joined the Bosnian defence forces and the family had managed to escape the Mostar death trap. Instead they had fled from village to village, finding shelter with friends and relatives, before moving on when the Serbs gathered for another attack.

Then, after many months of hiding and praying for survival, fate caught up with Admir. During a ramble in the woods near Stolac he was shot in the right leg, probably by hunters with shotguns. After initial treatment, the overstretched doctors at the nearby medical centre told Senada that they could do no more than patch up his gaping wounds.

Admir, small for his age and in agony, was left with a leg that healed into a twisted limb, still pocked with deep-seated shotgun pellets and likely to become increasingly useless as he grew.

He had become one of the Bosnian war's childhood statistics. But fate was about to take a hand once more in his life....

I had been staggered when I returned from Sarajevo in January, staggered by the money which had been donated by the newspaper's readers. Just over £60,000 was now in a special Bosnia appeal account. And, as the budget was finally totalled, it emerged that the surgeons' mission would cost far less than the estimated £20,000. In fact it amounted to less than £7,000, leaving a staggering £53,000 surplus. What a wonderful problem.

I was determined the money would be used wisely and for the purpose for which it was donated, to help the innocent victims of this cruel war. And who were more innocent than the children?

I wrote a newspaper story about children of war when I came back from Sarajevo. Its subject had moved me greatly. It concerned that day in the city when I had handed out chocolate to the boy and girl in the

Mandy O'Toole and the three elegant nurses, Sarajevo 1994

The 'Angel of Lipik' unloading the ambulance, with Allan Waller, the army driver, a nurse and the author, Lipik 1992

Graffiti, Mostar 1994

Cemetery, Sarajevo 1994

The BUPA plastic surgery team

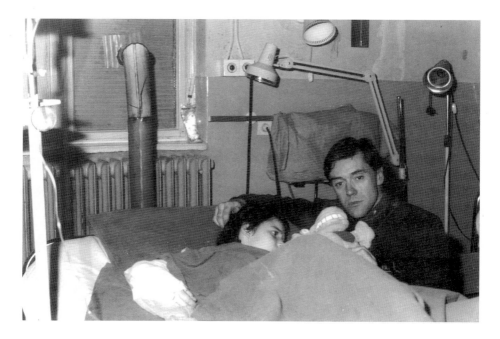

Kennan with 'Hector' and the author, Sarajevo 1994

Jasmine Longhurst amongst the toys, Norwich 1996

woolly winter hats and thick coats. They had joined dozens of other children who had been let out by anxious parents because the shelling and sniping had virtually stopped. And because they wanted to do what children love to do: play in the snow. They had wolfed down the chunky Lion bars in three bites. Then they had run off to make a slide on a nearby slope.

Minutes later I had been reminded of their innocence and vulnerability when I had narrowly escaped the bullets of a sniper who had not heard about a ceasefire.

The day after, as I was flying out to safety, a mortar crew slid a bomb down their tube. It arched up into the bright, white sky and came back to earth among a large group of children playing in the snow.

They called such impacts Sarajevo Roses because of the pretty petal patterns they left on the city's concrete pavements, through the twin effects of the high explosive and white-hot shrapnel. The heavier mortars were often aimed at crowded places. The world had been shocked by the scores killed in single explosions through direct hits on bread and water queues. This particular bomb killed six children and left more than a dozen cruelly injured. News pictures showed their blood in the ice and slush alongside one of their wooden toboggans. One picture showed a pack labelled 'USA refined vegetable oil' in the foreground close to the bloodied snow. In the propaganda war being fought by both sides, such an image would have singular resonance across the Atlantic. The Bosnians were desperate for American air power to be brought into play. Did someone place the pack, also bearing the stars and stripes emblem, on the ground? Did someone, other than the Serbs, fire that mortar? Such questions were not simply street talk throughout the city's siege. They were investigated at the highest levels. UN commanders and politicians argued over who fired the bomb. Troops were assigned to assess its trajectory, to estimate from which side of the front lines it had come.

As the argument and cynicism flared, the Pope condemned the atrocity. And six more black holes were being dug in the snow behind the Kosevo Hospital.

I was becoming increasingly angered by the callous duplicity of the power brokers and the military psychopaths. I was determined that if we could help anyone, no matter how few, then children would be our priority from now. The faces of those two, downing those chocolate bars, were etched in my memory. Had they been among the dead or injured? What were they doing now? What were the dead children's parents thinking? They had simply given in, like many parents, to the simple request 'to go outside and play in the snow'. After months of keeping their children imprisoned in apartments without proper heat or food, as the thunder had rocked their city, they had given in. And they had paid a price that would ruin their lives forever.

Such were the human realities behind the headlines, behind the semantics and deceptions of the politicians and military leaders. I knew that people were longing to identify with such minutiae. They could relate to individual children, parents and families; with their tragedy; with their heartbreak.

I knew by taking action and writing about it at the same time, I was blurring the lines increasingly between journalism as an impartial discipline, engaged in reportage of events, and a new pro-active journalism in which one becomes an active participant. I was doing what journalists traditionally never did: creating my own stories by stepping onto the stage. It was a moral dilemma which would trouble the BBC's Martin Bell constantly throughout the conflict. Eventually, it would force ITN's Michael Nicholson to take action, smuggling a Sarajevan orphan girl to Britain and eventually adopting her.

I had been determined to become as expert as possible on my chosen subject, reading every major work on Bosnian history and the latest books on the war. On an academic level, I was convinced of the rights of a multi-ethnic Bosnia Hercegovinia to determine its future as a democratically-led and independent state, free of the yoke of its Serbian oppressors. As a husband and a father, I was convinced that I had no option but to do what little I could to protect just a few of those innocent Bosnian children who would surely be dead before that dawn of freedom and independence rose above their tortured land.

There was a sense across Britain at that time of people looking for a channel for their frustrations over the mishandling of the war by Europe's leaders. Individuals and small groups were packing vans and trucks with aid and driving to the war looking for refugees. Some of the efforts were chaotic. People died behind the steering wheels of their vehicles, picked off by snipers or blown up by mines. Others blundered around Croatia and Bosnia with largely useless loads. Infamous among the foul-ups was the consignment of thousands of oil heaters delivered to snow-covered camps in southern Croatia, without any heating oil. And the hundreds of parcels sent to Bosnian Muslims, stamped, innocently, with the red star of a British parcel delivery company. Even desperate refugees rejected gifts bearing the same national symbol as that of the Serbs.

I could feel the pressure to act from regular calls and letters from the newspapers' readers. Even colleagues, hardened by years of journalism's diet of death and destruction, would begin conversations with: 'Well what are we doing next?' And it was the 'we' that was significant. People felt a part of what was being delivered through the power of a newspaper with one of the country's most loyal and generous readerships.

So I searched for someone who was making a difference purely for children. And I found David Southall. He was Professor of Paediatrics at Keele University and North Staffordshire Hospital in Stoke-on-Trent.

An energetic and sometimes controversial character, he had been a key figure in the evacuation to the UK of five-year-old Irma Hadzimuratovic the previous year. She was being treated at London's Great Ormond Street Children's Hospital for paralysis following shrapnel injuries and meningitis. Her case had become embroiled in acrimony because of the political fall-out which had surrounded her airlift. Warring factions were being accused of using such airlifts as 'bargaining chips' in a deadly game with the sponsoring powers. Despite such arguments, the end result was that a small girl with little chance of life was now being given some hope. I was certain that that was what really counted. Not the politics. Not the hatred. Not the media opportunities.

After extended discussions with David and his staff, it became clear that the Irma airlift was a media fixation. Working with the United Nation's Children's Fund, the Stoke team had a wide range of long and short term plans to help pulverised Mostar. Among its many needs was urgent medical help from outside experts. I wrote a story which included an appeal for doctors to help surgeons in the city's underground war hospital.

In all, more than 100,000 shells had turned the east bank Bosnian ghetto into a sea of rubble. Hardly a building was untouched. Most were now piles of the indigenous yellow stone which had given the ancient city such empathy with the surrounding hills. Some were marked by their surviving chimney stacks. Others were blackened hulks. Throughout those three years of hell, the war hospital had attempted to treat the maimed. Now its doctors were at breaking point. At this time, Bosnian and Croat forces in Bosnia had declared a ceasefire which had been taken up in Mostar. There the Bosnian enclave had survived largely because the local Croats were unwilling to fight street by street for the ghetto. The result would have been too bitter and costly for a force whose ethnic cleansing system elsewhere had mirrored the Serbs' technique of shelling, sniping and starving a population centre, before allowing the shattered women and children to leave as their menfolk were rounded up and taken to internment camps or execution sites.

The Serbs were also shelling less frequently, providing an opportunity to bring in doctors who could give some relief.

Norfolk General Practitioner Steve Main answered my newspaper plea. A tall, shy doctor in his forties, he was newly attached to a local practice and was doubling up with stints as a hospital anaesthetist. He was available, qualified and simply wanted to help. He was also a veteran of voluntary work for the International Red Cross on the Thai-Cambodia border.

With our appeal fund paying his costs, he flew out in early May for a planned three weeks of operations in the appalling conditions of the heavily shelled hospital. Doctors there regularly performed surgery on badly mutilated bodies under candlelight and with little water. Lack of beds also meant mothers, too, were having to leave just two hours after giving birth.

An ebullient Professor Southall was delighted we had found a volunteer. 'He's a hero,' he enthused. 'He has answered an emergency appeal at extremely short notice and has accepted the risks of going into a war zone.'

On his return, Steve was visibly moved by his experiences. Most people who undertook such missions made friends among the staff with whom they worked. I always found the people of the former Yugoslavia a colourful mix, from the cosmopolitan comedians and academics of Sarajevo to the insular and determined Croats of Lipik. Most of them possessed that Balkan predilection for alcohol to fuel deep and wide-ranging historical and philosophical conversations which could end in kisses or tears. In some ways, such unpredictable swings of emotion and logic were at the heart of their conflicts. The pale and gaunt doctor who sat before me had been touched by such idiosyncrasies when he related his experiences.

Just a few hours after touching down, he asked me: 'Have you seen the news? Have the Serbs started shelling yet? I was told they were about to begin again.

'One thing I achieved among these wonderful people was to make a lot of good friends who I am now very worried about.'

I assured him there had been no such news, as he told a harrowing story of his mission, which was marked by a pull-out by some Serb units. He had taken one particularly ironic photograph. It showed a toilet door at the doctors' accommodation in Mostar. At head height for anyone sitting on the loo, a collection of sniper's bulletholes was stitched across the green, ridged tin. Even the lavatory was a death trap in this city of such horrors.

In a calm, quiet voice, he described the scenes: 'The war hospital is really just a bomb-shattered building with sandbags up to the first floor and power only intermittently available, depending on there being any diesel to run the generators. It has taken quite a few hits. The windows are shored up with sandbags and props. The staff work in a dark, dingy basement. It is pretty grim, very battered, dark, and difficult to keep clean.

'Patients lie around in crowded wards, in beds with grey blankets. The operating theatre is a little room in the basement. You can only imagine what it was like during the heaviest shelling. It must have been horrendous. You were stuck down there with the knowledge that shells were being aimed at the hospital, which was a particular feature of the war.

'You were limited to emergency procedures, but all sorts of things are happening. We operated on gunshot wounds but we also removed an ovarian cyst from one woman, repaired hernias and several children were even circumcised.'

His work included stints in the war hospital and an attempt to set up a donated field hospital which had been sited three kilometres out of town.

'It's very difficult to get out there because of the lack of fuel. When the Serbs were actually in place they used to sit above the field hospital and shoot down on it. Basically, if you stuck your head outside you got shot at.

'They were able to control the road so you couldn't do anything with that hospital because the road was too exposed. It's fine now, but the fear is they will come back.'

The same went for the city centre, where shellshocked Bosnians were coming out to talk again.

'There's no shelling or shooting at present, but people are homeless and still afraid. They have been living in basements but there is not much rebuilding going on, mainly because people cannot believe the peace will last.

'There's a sense of shellshock in the town which was particularly evident in the doctors who are still operating in this siege mentality. Remarkable things were happening there, but they were reluctant to move out to the field hospital.

'At night Mostar is a spooky place, filled with the burned out shells of homes and offices. You walk down the street and almost bump into people who you can only see by the light of cigarettes or candles.

'By day it's crowded with people, most of whom are just milling around with nothing to do except carry water or pick up food. They sit and talk and drink a little vodka and coffee,

'People can tell you what happened. But they can't tell you why. They have heard all the arguments. But most people shake their heads and say it's crazy.'

Crazy indeed. This was a time when the Serbs had switched their efforts to rolling up the Bosnian eastern enclaves of Srebrenica, Zepa and Gorazde, bringing respite to Mostar. This window of relative peace gave the Stoke team the chance to implement another of their targets, the creation of a mobile health screening service in the city.

This would build up vital data on the state of health of the 120,000 people from all sides who were still alive after the phenomenal bombardment. It was a wonderfully unglamorous scheme. Following the controversy over the Irma airlift, it was unlikely to attract critical headlines from other media. It was simply not interesting enough for them. Yet it made sense to start the rebuilding of health services by assessing the crucial

requirements. Cholera, typhoid, TB and dysentery had either been discovered or rumoured to be present among a population who had been
unable to bury their dead properly and had drunk filthy water and eaten
rotten food frequently .

INTERLUDE

STOKE-ON-TRENT

The Stoke team were very adept at begging for aid. I admired their persistence and success in obtaining everything from free aircraft seats, hotel rooms and medical equipment to tonnes of baby food and the lorries to carry the shipments. In the end I identified two Applemac computers, a variety of eye, ear and blood-screening supplies and an Aloka portable baby scanner as our £20,000 contribution. The city's pregnant Bosnian women had no idea of the health of their unborn children. After the trauma and conditions they had endured, many could be carrying potentially fatal conditions. The £13,000 ultrasound scanner, bought at cost price, would be used to check for the first time on such problems.

I waved off the three-truck convoy on a wet May morning from Stoke's North Staffordshire Hospital, wondering what the next twist would be in our support for the embattled city. It came within weeks with an appeal from the Stoke team for an expert to help set up the medical laboratories which we had helped to equip.

By mid-October we had funded a mission by Alan Dean, a laboratory manager from Norfolk's main hospital, to spend a month in the city improving the number of medical samples the city's laboratories could handle. At present it was just fifty a day, a minor miracle after the pounding the system had suffered. He was used to 1,500 blood tests being done in his Norwich lab daily. But the friendly, fast-talking Londoner was realistic about what he could achieve, even with the equipment we had already sent.

'From what I understand, they have some very good technical equipment and people with the right training to use it. But what they haven't got is a proper system of organisation. Local doctors are just sending children to the labs with the requirements on a scrap of paper. The tests are being done and the results scribbled on the same bit of paper which the patients are taking back to the doctor.

'I honestly don't know how I am going to tackle the problems. If I try to put in the system we have here in Norwich, it almost certainly won't work. It's going to be a matter of getting back to basics and finding something that works, whatever the conditions are.'

He had little information on what he faced, including such advice as 'snipers usually miss'. And he confessed to having 'butterflies as big as aeroplanes' about venturing into the city. For long weeks, he toiled to bring in a workable new system which proved vital to rebuilding the basis of the city's shattered health services.

At the same time, the Serbs had turned their attentions onto the surrounding villages, where hundreds were killed that autumn in a systematic clearing operation. Among the thousands running for their lives were the Vele family. Little Admir Vele had been hit by a shotgun blast many months earlier. After initial treatment, his injury had not healed and he had been taken to the Mostar war hospital. There he was seen by Alan Dean: 'When I first saw his X-ray I thought it was just an awful X-ray, covered with specks. But it turned out to be lots of metal still in his leg. He wasn't a very happy chappie, but he is a lovely little fellow.'

I discussed his case in Stoke with David Southall, who was making regular and dangerous trips into Mostar and its surrounding towns and villages. He was hoping to organise an evacuation of children who did not meet the emergency criteria for life threatening conditions, but would be crippled or face ruined lives without outside medical attention.

I did not want the newspaper to get involved in an Irma-style slanging match with politicians and the other media. But these children were facing real tragedy. Some had serious bowel disorders or other complex conditions. Others, like Admir, had been shot or hit by shrapnel. Their local health service had broken down. Yet the humanitarian agencies had decided not to fly them abroad for treatment because they would not die. They would become progressively more crippled, possibly face amputation and agony in their teens. But they did not meet the criteria.

Well, that was not good enough. Why should Admir walk with a crutch or face a life with one leg because of rules drawn up in air-conditioned offices by well-heeled officials in aid agencies hundreds of miles from any war zone? If they wouldn't help, we had a moral duty to try.

I began private talks with the Norfolk and Norwich Hospital, which had done so much to help the Sarajevo mission and in releasing Alan Dean for his Mostar laboratory work.

The hospital trust's administration director, Richard Drew, was a former British Army colonel who shared my firm belief that we could not stand idly by in the face of the genocide in former Yugoslavia. Armed with UNICEF medical reports on Admir's condition, he discussed his prognosis with his consultants and fellow managers and concluded that the trust would be delighted to help.

The deal was hatched. The hospital would provide the treatment. Our appeal would cover transport and accommodation expenses.

Not only that, I agreed we would fund the flights of three other sick

Mostar children, aged from four to fifteen, together with their guardians. They would go to other medical centres across the UK. The total cost of the aircraft seats was just £2,500 in a special cut-price Lufthansa deal. It seemed a small price, alongside the millions which the international aid agencies had been pumping into their food and medical programmes. I was always amazed at the luxury which surrounded their staff in the war zone. Often travelling in top-of-the-range Land Cruisers, some would sport satellite telephone links and car-borne coffee machines. Many were dedicated and skilled professionals. But some were obvious career-building war tourists, resplendent in gold-rimmed Ray Bans and designer fatigues. They seemed to be intent on improving their CVs with short stays in Sarajevo or Tuzla. These were the same people who would draw up criteria banning desperately sick children from airlifts.

I travelled from Norwich in an ambulance to pick up Admir from Heathrow airport, where the Stoke team had managed to book the whole party, free of charge, into the luxury Ramada hotel, off the perimeter road. A senior manager there just happened to be a Bosnian.

Admir was a cute boy, with huge brown eyes that were bound to woo the doctors and nurses. His mother Senada and his younger brother, three year old Adnan were with him. So too was the bubbly Stoke doctor, Jill Ellis, who was still as fresh as a daisy after accompanying the party on their long car drive from Mostar to Split, followed by three separate flights.

Jill hugged a smiling Admir, who was cuddling a symbolic yellow football, and told me: 'The kids have been absolutely incredible on the journey. They cried a bit when they were exhausted, but they have been completely overwhelmed by what they have seen so far.'

As the party split up and each little group went off to different parts of Britain, we headed for Norwich.

INTERLUDE

NORFOLK

On the way to Norwich, Senada, through an interpreter I had arranged, told me her heart-rending story.

She had seen and done things which no mother should ever have to face. She had heard her two children crying for days with hunger which she could do nothing to subdue. She had seen her husband, Muhammed, return from a concentration camp. He was a living skeleton she thought, and must surely die. And now she was having to accept the charity of strangers in a foreign land to give her first-born son the chance to save him from lifelong disablement.

It was little wonder that the exhausted and bewildered young woman was quick to cry, her eyes clouding with emotion as she recounted the horrors of her past life.

It had been very different when, as a teenager, she had married Muhammed, her childhood sweetheart, in Stolac, a town in the rolling hills south of Mostar. He worked on the land, she was employed in the textile industry, and the future looked bright. They had a comfortable home and lifestyle. Then came the Serb onslaught of the previous year. Muhammed had been fighting with the defence force when he had been captured and interned for months.

His recent release revealed him to be too weak to travel far. In between, Senada had struggled to keep herself and the children alive, changing homes four times, each time fleeing before the invaders arrived to level the homes and slaughter those too ill or frightened to leave.

Through tear-filled black eyes, she told me: 'The worst thing for us has been the hunger. For four days at one time we had no food at all, no bread, nothing for the children.

'When the shelling got too bad, we fled from the house and left everything we owned behind. One time we had to survive for two months on two kilos of flour. I made tiny pieces of bread and sometimes could help other people. Adnan, my little one, used to cry from hunger.

'It's different now, we receive some food and have managed to stretch it out to make ends meet. But the worst thing is that there is no money. You can buy things now, but not if you have no money.

'I worry always about the children. I try not to let them out and am

46

afraid for them. A lot of children have died just because they have gone out to play.

'Adnan has only known war in his life. Whenever he hears a loud bang he thinks it is grenades coming in. In the beginning it was hard for them to sleep. But now they are used to it.' Their present home, a one-bedroom apartment in Potoci village, was very close to the front line, but quieter since the ceasefire. Even so, it was considered too dangerous for visiting British doctors to call on them before they left for Heathrow.

And so it was, just three weeks before Christmas, 1994, that the Vele family were given a gift of kindness they could never have imagined.

Within twenty-four hours, Admir had been assessed and was in the operating theatre at the Norfolk and Norwich Hospital. There, orthopaedic consultants John Albert and A. D. Patel used advanced techniques to reset his badly injured leg. The initial fracturing caused by the gunshot had been treated satisfactorily, but the lack of follow-up help had caused deformity. The scarring from the soft tissue injury was believed to have been acting like a bowstring on the leg and preventing the bone from healing properly. The doctors anticipated this bowing would have worsened as the leg grew. It would probably never have healed properly, with Admir facing pain and deformity as he got older. The splintered leg was now held in place by a Circular Ilizarov apparatus, a £2,000 Russian invented cage, comprising steel wires, rods and bolts to maintain position and stability.

The shower of lead pellets which showed up on his X-ray were there, left alone, as is standard procedure, to avoid the far more harmful damage involved in their removal. In effect, Admir would carry them round for life without any serious side effects, apart from possibly setting off airport metal detectors.

But there was a good chance of a full recovery. Admir, the boy crippled by war had not been filed for life in the non-emergency category of the aid agencies. He might well play his beloved football once more.

Senada was overjoyed. Along with Adnan, the hospital had arranged for her to stay with Admir during the early stages of his recovery. We knew the strengthening and physiotherapy work might take up to two months. I needed to find a home for the family, as well as transport and an interpreter to help the doctors with their questions during outpatient visits. It seemed a tall order. But I have always been amazed at the power of a newspaper appeal in solving such problems.

Tanja Bone, thirty, who graduated in English from Sarajevo University, had already acted as an interpreter and was now prepared to offer the home she shared with her boyfriend Andrew Bone, thirty-five.

The former ice cream salesman had been so disturbed by the scenes he had seen of the war that he had applied to drive aid lorries to Tuzla, Zenice and Banja Luca. In Sarajevo, he had met Tanja, fallen in love and managed to bring her back to Norfolk, where they were working through the tortuous naturalisation process for her and planned to marry shortly.

'They are from my country and are in distress and need help,' said Tanja. 'It was Andrew who phoned the *EDP* after he had taken me for a driving lesson and saw the article when he bought the newspaper.

'I agreed with him. I didn't hesitate. They will be utterly, utterly bewildered. If you have seen the pictures from Mostar you will know what it is like.

'I am looking forward to taking them on the market to show the children the sweets, to see their eyes, their expressions at such things.

'Admir is old enough to have known such things before the war started. But you can imagine what they have been through. They have experienced the worst period of the war and are still alive.'

It was a huge boost. I was able to offer to cover their expenses from our fund and Tanja, who was not able to work yet, would be available round-the-clock to help the Veles through the trauma of living in a land where they faced a foreign culture and spoke little English.

From the first two days, it was clear that the family had long been starved of the luxuries they found in the hospital's Laura Stuart children's ward. When Admir woke from his operation, he was quick to join Adnan in front of the television cartoons, giggling and joking along despite their lack of understanding. The food, too, was eagerly wolfed down by the two boys who were both slightly underweight for their age after many months of hardship.

Admir was a sheer delight. It would have been difficult to have found a boy more likely to have burrowed his way into the affections of everyone he encountered. He was bright, cheeky, inquisitive and with a smile for all the journalists, photographers and TV crews who passed through in those early days. He became a media opportunity.

Senada was more of a worry. Sullen, forcing a smile for the cameras, she was pining for her husband and her home, despite the war. She always supplied the right kind of quote, via Tanja, for visiting interviewers.

One of her first answers was: 'I have a lot of emotions. I thought the operation wouldn't be successful, but when I heard everything was fine, I was absolutely thrilled. The staff are really, really nice and I thank them.'

Behind the smile was a homesickness that would come very close to overwhelming this bewildered young woman, who had seen such horrors and shown such courage in keeping her children alive for so many months. She missed Muhammed deeply. But she was torn between presenting a face of gratitude to her benefactors and longing to return to him.

She was uplifted by the rapid progress being made by Admir. Just two days after his operation, he stood up for the first time and wiggled his toes. His room already showed some of the signs of his presence. On one wall was a brightly coloured drawing of a house, signed 'Admir Vele, Bosna Hercegovina'. Presents had been pouring in from across the country, toys, games and books in the main. One turned up that afternoon, brightly wrapped, sent in by a child whose injured leg had also been corrected by the hospital. Before he ripped off the paper cover, Admir's attention was grabbed by a large metal paperclip attached to the accompanying card. Laughing excitedly, he played with the clip, like so many children tend to do. The big teddy in the box would have to wait.

Five days later, Admir was making his first entrance back into the big, wide world, for a very special occasion. He was guest of honour at the wedding of Tanja and Andrew and stepped out of his small wheelchair to walk, proudly and without help into the register office. The city's Jarrolds department store had dressed him for the occasion. He was sporting a smart navy blue polo-neck, mustard waistcoat, trendy denim jacket, with white carnation, and navy jogging pants covering the metal frame which was still supporting his right leg.

That day, he also left the children's ward and the family joined their newlywed hosts at their leased cottage in pretty Reepham, near Norwich. It was to be a special event, with Tanja cooking real Bosnian pita, made of filo pastry filled with potatoes and spices.

And so it was to be. Over the next two months, Tanja and Andrew looked after the family's every need, from trying to keep Senada's spirits up with familiar dishes, to driving Admir to and from physiotherapy sessions.

Psychologically, the shock of adjustment was deep and unpredictable. Sometimes Adnan would show anger for no apparent reason. Sleep did not always come easily for any of them. And Senada appeared to be developing that lethargy which suggests depression. She was now chain-smoking, which was difficult for non-smoking Tanja and Andrew, and had become hooked on television soaps, despite not knowing the language.

The signs were symptoms of the torment they were all still suffering. Through Tanja, she opened her heart about the wave of killing and destruction which had swept through their young lives, declaring defiantly: 'I have managed to get through that period and we have stayed alive. I'm afraid of nothing now.'

The frightened questions of her two sons still surfaced in that comfortable pink-washed cottage in an historic Norfolk street.

'Whenever they hear a strange sound or loud noise, they are afraid it has started again. They ask about the basement and where they can hide.

'I tell them they do not have to fear. There is no shooting or shelling here. But they are worried about their father and ask: 'What has happened to dad?'

'They remember how horrible it was. We would wake in the morning and there was always fear. The children would be indoors all the time and they did not have anything to eat. We had to manage as well as we could. If you had money, you had to spend it all on food because it was so expensive. I did not really eat at that time. I would save all the food for my children.'

At the height of the conflict around Mostar, a 25-kilo sack of flour was costing more than £40, when many families had lost everything. Senada managed to hide some savings in Admir's bandages as they fled through the hills. And she had to listen as the boys cried themselves to sleep with hunger.

'One day I took Admir to Mostar for a change of dressings. In the morning I gave him a small piece of bread, and when we arrived in the hospital he saw food being given to the patients and asked if they were going to give him some. But they didn't and he was crying because he was hungry all the way home.

'Now they both prefer bread and potatoes to meat. This little one (Adnan) was born to no meat, so it means nothing to him. The other one (Admir), he has forgotten.'

There were many high points. The local community rallied round magnificently. All three pubs in the small town raised money to help. Parties were held and there were countless gifts and trips arranged.

The Rotary club arranged for Admir to be guest of honour at the Norwich Theatre Royal pantomime. He knew the story of Aladdin in that wonderful children's network that makes so many of their fairy tales universal. If only adults could communicate so easily. There were also the Dinosaur Park, the Puppet Theatre and trips round toy shops.

Six weeks later, Tanja and Andrew asked me if I could arrange a break for them. They had experienced a very intensive period of caring for the Veles. There had been many interviews, journeys, torments for the children as well as joys. There had also been cultural issues. On one occasion, Tanja had had to take a hand when Senada had stepped out into the garden, broken a stick from a bush and returned inside to declare that she was about to beat the boys for an episode of bad behaviour. That kind of discipline, Tanja, had told her, was not allowed in Britain these days. And she had taken the stick from her.

On top of such pressures, the couple had hardly had any time alone together since their wedding. I opted for my usual appeal for help in the newspaper. A kind local family immediately stepped in. The Veles enjoyed a change of scenery and more trips to exciting local venues. And the Bones had a much deserved weekend of blissful solitude.

Then, three months after his arrival, Admir was declared fit enough to return home. The steel cage was removed from his leg in late February and he was walking and even running without help. Doctors worked out a continuing programme of treatment, including physiotherapy. But it was doubtful that the health services of Mostar would be able to cope for some time with such secondary care.

In truth, everyone was hoping that the work done in Norfolk and his natural zest and vitality would be enough to see him through. He had been given the best chance available for his once-shattered leg to grow into a straight and sturdy limb.

There were many goodbyes and expressions of gratitude. Tanja spoke movingly: 'It brings tears to your eyes to see a little boy walking normally and remembering how he was. His leg was all bent, it was horrible. Now it's a proper leg and he walks.'

And, as the nurses had their final cuddles with the little man in the new denim jacket, my good friend, administrator Richard Drew, spoke volumes for the whole hospital: 'It's been a pleasure to see such a vast improvement in a little boy who, through no fault of his own, was injured. He came in a wheelchair and he has now walked back out and is heading home. What better present could we give him?'

Senada had broken into her first natural smile since I had told her the flight from Heathrow was fixed. She said: 'I came here knowing nobody. I was a complete stranger and now my son is cured. I am so grateful.'

Next day, I joined the family at the Heathrow Ramada Hotel, where Dr Jill Ellis and some of the other Stoke team members had gathered to take home the Veles and some of the other evacuated children who had also had the best treatment the National Health Service could offer.

As the children filled their new rucksacks with the stacks of donated presents that were still pouring in, I shook hands with Senada and wished her well. She began to cry and hugged me hard, speaking in an impenetrable stream of quickfire Bosnian. I kissed little Adnan and turned to find Admir. He was already heading for the door. When he reached it, he turned, shouted my name, stuck up the thumb on his right hand, then turned again and was gone.

That was Admir Vele. Going home. To play football.

IV

IT STARTED ROUTINELY ENOUGH

Sarajevo Diary – March 1995

It started routinely enough. In bright sunshine, we were standing outside Sarajevo's once-glamorous Holiday Inn, exchanging greetings with a friend.

Then the first shots rang out.

They were fired from the ugly grey high rises, a couple of hundred metres away across the Milacka river. They were followed by the sound of glass shattering on a tram as it headed into the nearby terminus.

People were screaming.

More shots. Single sniper rounds. More glass shattered. The noise of tram wheels screeching and grinding hard on steel rails.

Then a heavier weapon started its gut-churning thudding. It was a 30 millimetre cannon on top of a white UN armoured vehicle parked just off the main road. Positioned behind huge steel plates, it was intended as a deterrent to the snipers. The French Foreign Legionnaire gunner's blue helmet could be seen shaking with the vibrations of its fearsome black barrel. Each time he fired, a crown of orange and white flame belched outward.

We watched the action briefly, but maintained our composure. There is a rule in these situations. You follow the example of the most experienced person in your group. Our friend was a dignified late middle-aged banker who had lived in the city all his life. He was continuing with our conversation. So we feigned disinterest in the action to our left. Gifts were exchanged. We even discussed having a coffee in the hotel foyer.

Then more snipers opened up. The air around us suddenly filled with the sound of large bees. Dozens of them. These were bullets whipping past us. They were followed by the slower moving thumping sound of the weapons which had fired them. Experienced soldiers will tell you that the gap between the buzz and the thump signifies how close they are flying past you.

These were virtually instantaneous.

My composure suddenly deserted me. I grabbed my rucksack and ran forty metres through what felt like a thick swarm of bees gyrating around me in a heavy hailstorm. I made for the cover of the hotel walls. Once there, I hugged the yellow plasterwork, breathing deeply, cold sweat trickling down my forehead. I dared not even look out to check how the battle was going.

At a more dignified pace, my companions joined me. Even they broke into a trot over the final few metres.

We went for that coffee. Followed by another.

Strong and black …

Something had told me I would be back in Sarajevo at some time. The thought was disturbing. The city was a potential death trap where your fate was outside your control. As the MSF security man had warned, if you could see surrounding hills, the snipers could see you. And every time you walked the streets, you could see the hills.

But there was also so much that could be done there, particularly for its children.

The seeds of my return were planted back in the previous autumn. I had been in touch with Colonel Mark Cook, who had rebuilt the gutted orphanage in Lipik, the scene of our Christmas Convoy mission. I had been told he had left the Army after thirty-two years as a Gurkha officer and was setting up a new charity, Hope and Homes for Children.

The aim, with his wife Caroline, was to create homes for children around the world who had been caught up in the horrors of wars or civil or natural disasters. Mark was born at Earsham, in Norfolk and close enough to be claimed by the local newspaper as 'a local boy'. His family had run a butcher's business in nearby Gorleston and he had started his education in Southwold.

He had also shown his determination in Croatia, managing to fund the £1 million reconstruction project from voluntary subscriptions whilst still serving as the commander of the British UN Protection Force in the country.

At their pretty L-shaped home in a Wiltshire village, the Cooks set about their task. Caroline the cool administrative head. Mark the energetic, creative charmer.

They had married young, in 1967. Caroline was a trained nanny, Mark then already a dashing young Gurkha officer. They travelled extensively, and have two sons, Edward and William. 'It would have been lovely to have more,' said Caroline later. 'I always thought four would have been nice. But we had a smashing life. We swung from Hong Kong to Germany to Penang to Malaya, Gurkhas waiting on us hand and foot.'

In twenty-five years, they moved home eighteen times, packing up the children's things, leaving friends, making more, beginning new challenges each time. As Mark approached retirement, the house in Wiltshire appeared the ultimate nest, the dream of a couple who had passed through so much Army accommodation for so long. But the horrors of Croatia stirred Mark to action. He had expected the Lipik project to cost around £250,000. When it was estimated professionally at £1 million, friends told him to walk away from such an unachievable target.

Among them, BBC corresondent Martin Bell, also born near Earsham and a fellow pupil of the Leys School in Cambridge, was adamant: 'It seemed an impossible task.'

Then came the big break. Mark flew to Sarajevo to see the BBC man. Just before the lunchtime bulletin, a mortar bomb exploded close by. A piece of shrapnel hit Bell in the groin, the incident captured dramatically on camera. As the satellite link with London came on the line, Mark took over the slot and told BBC viewers about the injury and the Lipik orphanage project. It was the best free advertisement he could have hoped for. Cheques began to flow in and major partnerships emerged, not least a £100,000 donation from Baroness Chalker, on behalf of the Overseas Development Administration. By Christmas, 1993, Mark had delivered his promise to open the home and had resigned his commission. I had written a number of articles about the Lipik project and Mark had been in touch to thank the newspaper's readers for their generosity. Their cheques had also poured in.

Now, with Caroline, he was launching the new charity, and their first aim was to rebuild Sarajevo's main orphanage, a stinking hovel which had been turned into a partial ruin by deliberately aimed mortars and rockets.

It seemed like the perfect project for some of the Operation Sarajevo appeal fund surplus. It was about children, Sarajevo and 'a local boy', albeit via Hong Kong and Wiltshire, was the key figure. Mark and Caroline were delighted when I turned up at their London charity book launch with a £20,000 cheque. It was presented by the operating theatre manager from the Operation Sarajevo team, Mandy O'Toole, who had become a good friend. She spoke movingly of her experiences in what we had called 'hell city'. She also told of her hopes that the money would help provide the orphans with a decent new home.

It was one of those peculiarly London events. One or two national tabloid journalists turned up looking for scandal. Michael Nicholson, the ITN veteran correspondent was there. He had become a firm backer of the scheme, having rescued and adopted orphan Natasha from the home. But the fickle finger of news management had swung against the event. That same morning, most media attention was focused on a rather different launch, that of Anna Pasternak's controversial book on James Hewitt's kiss-and-tell account of his relationship with Princess Diana. There was no competition.

Undaunted, the Cooks ploughed on, working virtually round the clock on promoting and setting up the charity and the Sarajevo project. The couple had already visited the three-storey orphanage twice and were shocked by the conditions.

The Ljubice Ivezic home was high on a hill on the north-eastern fringe of the city, a prominent target for the surrounding Serb gunners. Its history was chequered. Built with Titoesque architectural values, its exterior was drab, turreted concrete. Inside it was a dingy warren of windowless corridors, with numerous bedrooms, most for several children to share. Its position had made it a partial ruin. The explosions had blown out most windows, sliced huge holes in the roof and forced the children into the stinking, sewage-covered basement during the heavier bombardments. One *Sunday Times* correspondent described the home as 'the worst place in Sarajevo after the morgue'. So poor were conditions that scores of children were evacuated in coach convoys two years earlier to families in Italy and Germany. That left forty-four children aged from a few months to eighteen years, each of them alone in the world. Some were illegitimates, who were shunned by the authoritarian former Communist regime. Others were economic orphans, dumped by parents made penniless by the war. Most were true orphans, whose parents had been killed or were now missing.

As Mark explained: 'The children are living almost like animals. The food is appalling. None of them are going to school and nobody is looking after them. The whole thing is in ruins, even the floorboards and doors were ripped out for firewood and the children are just existing.

'There is one particular baby whose single mother has been turned out onto the street because, at twenty-two, she is considered too old to live there.'

The aim was to rebuild the home, then send in expert volunteers to provide motivation for the children and some development for their futures.

Surveys and contracts had already been started. One of the charity's key policies was to use local labour and materials in any project. That helped local employment and generated affinity with the charity among the population. The next step in Sarajevo was to fly in and negotiate a deal with the city construction companies, as well as establishing a legal and financial structure for the scheme. Mark invited me to join him there. I owed it to the people who had sent in their cheques, postal orders and cash to show them first-hand how their hard-earned money was being spent. But the prospect had a profound effect on me. My wife June was building up her interiors business, which meant we were apart much of the time. She had been very supportive, but occasionally expressed her fears. She also saw how Jared and Janna had been affected. The first Sarajevo trip had been surrounded by a blaze of publicity. The children were being questioned regularly by friends. But I had decided to tell them as much as possible about what it was like and, more importantly, why I was going. I described individual children in the orphanage. Mark had given me enough information on some of them for their tragedy to become personal, individual, with names and descriptions. Like Admir Vele, these were children just like my own. Not faces flashing by on a television screen.

It was enough to convince them the risks were worthwhile. Increasingly their worries were displaced by an unspoken, but obvious pride in what was being done. This was their dad, doing something good. That was the message I repeated to them regularly.

And that was why I was able to take myself back again to our 'city of hell'.

It had been over a year since the surgical mission there. Bosnian Serbs had continued grinding out their quota of death in a meaningless daily routine. At the same time as the two sides pounded each other's front-line bunkers, the Serb gunners continued to concentrate some of their attentions on the city's streets. The aim was to disrupt the life of the capital with the terrorism of attrition.

The Serbs might well have been powerful enough in armour and artillery to capture the city, but a shortage of manpower would have prevented them from holding it. Their leader, Radovan Karadzic, also knew it would be a Pyrrhic victory, the resulting humanitarian disaster bringing them world condemnation. It was, he judged, far better to continue with their established routine of siege and slaughter there whilst concentrating military efforts on gaining territory in the less publicised eastern enclaves and elsewhere. As a result, ceasefires had come and gone in Sarajevo, often being used to relieve and resupply stretched units on both sides of the front lines. Even these had been breached regularly. And the humanitarian airlift had been suspended and restarted each time chunks had been knocked out of a transport plane by apparently desultory ground fire.

All this was occupying my mind when Mark and I strapped ourselves into the jump seats of the big green, four-engined RAF Hercules on the flightline at Split Airport. Next stop Sarajevo. We could not help remembering that it had been an Italian Hercules that had been shot out of the sky by a ground-launched rocket on the same route. Yet the courageous young flight crews at the former Croatian holiday resort were determined to make as many sorties as possible.

There remained an air of unreality about what was happening. I almost had to pinch myself back into the world as I gazed out of a side window. An internal flight had just landed and grey and blue-suited businessmen were stepping down, heading off for a day in the city with their black leather briefcases and grey raincoats in their hands. For Croatia, business was getting back to normal.

Instead, we were heading off for a week in one of the most dangerous places on earth. Stop the world, I thought, I want to get off.

As the plane punched through the thin clouds, we rechecked our gear. I was designated as the Assistant Director of Hope and Homes for Children, a title enscribed on the vital UNHCR Blue Card hanging like a dogtag around my neck. The position gave me more sway with the people we would be meeting. Anyway, I still had my international Press card available if I needed it. My rucksack included the normal collection of cold weather clothing and thick duck-down sleeping bag which I had taken in before. I had also loaded up with a stock of ready-cook meals. Food supplies were very unpredictable and we would have to fend for ourselves in the city centre apartment which Mark had rented on previous trips. I was also wearing a very heavy, borrowed, bullet-proof jacket. It had a ceramic chest insert, as before. But there was also a high collar which was added protection against what UN troops had noticed had become one of the Serb sniper's favourite targets, the neck. I took some consolation from this improvement on my chances of survival. What I hadn't considered was exactly why the neck shot was so common among peacekeepers. The reason was that it represented that vulnerable unprotected gap between the top of their ordinary armoured jackets and their helmet. The fact that I didn't have a helmet on this trip meant that the collar was probably an irrelevance. They had my whole, unprotected head to shoot at. Still, hindsight is a wonderful science.

Our fellow passengers on the aid flight included a clutch of UN soldiers and two attractive, teenage girls, who claimed to be Croatian journalists. When the aircrew offered a view of the flight deck it was on condition that those accepting had what one of them described as 'two perfectly formed assets'. That encompassed the girls. But it excluded Mark and I.

Eventually, we were asked to come forward and were given a briefing on what lay ahead. The blonde-haired pilot, chisel-jawed in gold rimmed aviator sunglasses, was gripping the throttle with yellow chamois gloves, as he told us that the Khe Sanh manoeuvre was still being used by the RAF to avoid groundfire on landing at Sarajevo. Unlike the low-level approach preferred by the Russians on my last trip, this was the high-altitude dive created by the Americans during the Vietnam war. US transport planes had suffered such high casualties on the way in and out of their big Khe Sanh base that they opted for a very high approach, followed by tight turns then a near-vertical dive toward the runway.

The subsequent sharp pull-up of the lumbering, loaded beast comes just in time to make a safe landing.

Mark had already experienced the treat. He grinned at my look of consternation as I strapped myself tightly into the jump seat again.

When the dive came, it was worse than I had expected. Like the steepest roller-coaster downcurve I have ever experienced, it left my breakfast and main internal organs somewhere behind me. The engines screamed, the airframe vibrated, and I was left to calculate the total mass of the lashed-in load of food and medical supplies that stood a few centimetres from my face. All I could contemplate was the size of the hole we would be making in the ground below. That, and the sounds of the rockets and bullets which I was certain I could hear flashing past as the gunners in their bunkers alongside the airfield attempted to ensure we had a very bad day.

I need not have worried. The RAF crews on this run regularly trained with special forces, performing similar manoeuvres as a matter of routine. And, fortunately, contrary to my suspicions, the airport Serbs were having a lie-in.

The big aircraft seemed to be popping rivets, groaning with stress and pain, as it levelled out. So was my stomach. Through the window, the hills that had been specks below, were now above us. I was looking up at the bedroom windows of bombed-out villas as we roared in at near-zero altitude. Then we were down, hard, without a bounce, on the runway. The sad bulk of a crashed Illyushin transport plane flashed by. Within seconds our engines were bursting into reverse thrust and my remaining dental fillings appeared to be working themselves loose.

The aircraft lurched to a sharp halt. Mark and I unclipped ourselves. The RAF loadmaster indicated a side door. We thanked him, loaded our gear and were down on the pock-marked concrete, running toward the sandbags and steel containers protecting the arrivals area.

Sarajevo felt different in the March sunshine. Almost civilised. There had been a ceasefire operating since New Year's Day. It had been broken almost daily. And it was only after we hitched a lift with an aid team and saw the destruction of no-man's land that we were reminded of where we were.

Outside the Holiday Inn, Hilma, the banker, stepped out to greet us. Then the shooting had started and we fled inside for our strong coffees.

Hilma, tall and distinguished with white-hair and a grey coat, had then summoned a taxi by telephone to take us into the city centre. When the man arrived in an ageing yellow Yugo, he was beside himself with fear. He had gunned the car over the hotel's car park barrier, onto the grass surround, ending up with his bonnet in the foyer doorway. Out he leapt, running inside, blurting out a stream of Bosnian curses.

Hilma told us the man had narrowly escaped the firefight on Sniper Alley and was refusing to take us back down there.

I had always been told that things were getting really risky in Sarajevo when the taxi drivers refuse a fare. I wondered if this was some kind of bargaining technique. But the man's shaking hands looked genuine enough.

As Hilma insisted, the price rose. And for thirty Deutschmarks – just over £13 and many months salary for most people in the city – the driver suddenly nodded his approval and the three of us dived into the battered Communist-built saloon. Reversing out of the foyer entrance, the driver swung round the side of the glass and concrete hotel, using its huge bulk as cover from the gun battle that was still in progress to our left. Building speed painfully slowly, we circled the hotel and entered the dual carriageway into town and along Sniper Alley. Ahead we could see the white UN armoured vehicle firing into the multi-storey apartment blocks, in the Serb-controlled district of Grbavica, on the opposite bank of the river to our right. A clutch of blue-helmeted soldiers were watching from the cover of the tall steel shields nearby.

As the engine whined frighteningly, we were suddenly out in the open, nearing the UN vehicle, where bullets were kicking up dirt. And we were alone. Not a car or pedestrian could be seen. I was in the right hand-side of the back seat of the left-hand drive car. I suddenly became aware I would be passing closest to the action.

Strange how such selfish thoughts occur in moments of deep stress. I had pulled my rucksack up against the side window, hoping, probably with undue optimism, that the heavy sleeping bag, ready-cook meals and camera gear might absorb or deflect any bullets. I noticed Mark had done the same with his smaller bag alongside me.

Then the driver, at what must have been 90 kilometres an hour, put his head down between his knees and appeared to be praying. I imitated the manoeuvre and noticed that Hilma, in the front seat, and Mark had done the same, alongside me.

For what seemed like minutes, but was actually seconds, we were barrelling along, at high speed, past the firefight with a driver who was studying his footwear. The sound of the UN cannon was ear-shattering. The sound of the occasional bullet whipping past the glassless car windows was less threatening, but more sinister, above the whine of the straining engine.

Then the driver swore what must have been a Bosnian oath of joy, lifted his head, regained control and we were safe, in the protective shadow of a collection of heavily damaged apartment blocks on our side of the river. He chattered excitedly. Hilma, like a veteran of such incidents, asked if we were alright. Naturally, we replied in the affirmative. After all, Brits like us would hardly be rattled by such trifling experiences. Privately, I was doubtful. My mind was fixed on the recuperative effects that a stiff glass of malt whisky might deliver. But I never mentioned the point.

The taxi crossed the river and pulled up at our apartment block. He seemed to have recovered from his experiences. His mood lifted when Mark handed over the German banknotes. and he began to offer us a deal for the rest of the week. For the same amount he would drive us wherever we wanted to go. It seemed a bargain. But I began to wonder if the Sniper Alley fare had been a little over the odds. His fear had appeared genuine. Surely he did not make a habit of ducking his head for long periods whilst operating the steering wheel. Unconvinced, we took his phone number and promised we would call if we needed a driver.

Our rooms were midway up an old, solidly-built block in the centre of town. Mark had rented them cheaply from an elderly Bosnian couple. They lived in their other rooms upstairs. He was the retired manager of a construction company and greeted me with assurances that the block would survive the heaviest of mortar or shells. It was heartening to know the apartment block would survive.

But what about us?

Inside, the flat was a turn-of-the-century affair: spacious, with two large rooms, with beds and a small kitchen. It was cluttered with old furniture and the belongings of the couple's daughter, a bright student in her early twenties, who was staying upstairs with them during our trip. One of the apartment's main attractions was its position, within easy walking distance of most of our key contacts. Its windows, too, were not overlooked by any of the surrounding hills. A small point, but one which attains great daily significance in a city where so many had died by presenting themselves as a tempting target behind a pane of glass or transparent plastic sheeting.

We unpacked quickly, Hilma returned and we were driven back over the river and up to the orphanage.

Bjelave is the steep hill from which the Ivezic home derives its name. It was one of the most exposed areas of the city, heavily shelled by the Serb positions on the higher ground to the east and west. The brick and concrete shape of the home looked even more forbidding than in the photographs I had seen. Its grey and yellow walls were pockmarked with bullet and shrapnel holes. Most of the windows had been blown out. A black scar marked one wall where fire had raged for a time. Outside the grounds were littered with stinking household rubbish, some of it spilling from an old skip.

A group of older children walked over to greet the car. As we stepped out, a boy of no more than twelve, smiled and asked if I had any cigarettes. Others pulled at my sleeve, mimicking the act of smoking, looking every inch the urchins they had become.

Inside, we mounted the black and dingy staircase to the bedrooms. Water covered the ground floor. There was little light on the upstairs corridor, just the pervasive stench of rotting garbage and damp.

The bedrooms were equally dark and, despite the sunshine outside, very cold, their UNHCR-stamped plastic sheeting fluttering and shredded. In one room, at the end of the corridor, sat a teenage boy on a single chair. Light from the bright sky above his head was punching through the shell-hole in the roof. It danced upon his head, picking out the angry scar from the shrapnel wound which had damaged his brain and nearly killed him.

Nearby was the baby room, the warmest in the building. Here nine orphan babies and toddlers were living communally with untrained staff trying to meet their needs. The heat was coming from an ageing gas-fired contraption in the centre of the room. Mark showed me its dangers. Like so many others in this make-and-mend city, its energy came from a gas pipe which produced an open flame. This roared without a guard, also heating the metal casing to a blistering level. Even more serious, was the lack of a cheap valve on the pipe which would increase its combustion efficiency and reduce levels of dangerous carbon monoxide fumes. This was all in a room filled with babies and toddlers.

One woman told us everyone hoped there would not be a tragedy before new heaters arrived at some point in the future. She shrugged when asked when.

It was the same picture all over the building. Desperation. After almost 1,000 days of war, the forty-four children left at the home were mostly desperate for love and affection and frightened for their futures. Their lives had improved a little from the dark days of the winter of 1992/3 when the city feared it would be overrun and a massacre would ensue. That was when people had burned some of the home's floorboards, doors and furniture to save the children from freezing to death during the heaviest shelling and sniping. For as many as three days and nights at a time, the children had been taken to the dark, damp, stinking cellar where they had screamed in terror as ordnance had rained down on surrounding tenements, schools and the nearby Kosevo Hospital. At that time there had been more than fifty babies there, each needing up to five nappy changes a day. The struggle had been virtually impossible. Yet the collection of largely untrained and lowly-paid staff, had managed to keep most of the children safe. Three children had been wounded, the worst being a small blonde-haired girl whose left ear had been torn off by a sniper round.

In the end, the world had demanded action. Coachloads of children were evacuated from the home to Italy and Germany. Two were shot dead by Serb gunmen during the journeys; nine were kidnapped.

Those now surrounded by love and relative luxury in the homes of Italian and German families were the lucky ones, selected for their adaptability to their new surroundings. The forty-four who were now living in this sub-Dickensian hovel, had lost out once more in the cruel lottery of life. Some came from homes broken by the same social pathology which strikes families in any country: abandonment, poverty, illegitimacy and imprisonment. Some were also complete orphans. Their parents had become statistics of death; memories; fading photographs in their grubby rucksacks.

It was no wonder that some reached out for attention, adopted grudging attitudes to offers of help, stole, fought and vandalised their way through a cruel life. Their torment had moved British Independent Television News correspondent Michael Nicholson so deeply that he had smuggled one small waif, Natasha, back to England. He had since formalised her adoption and she was growing up, as a pretty, well-balanced teenager in the Nicholson's family home. In a moving diary account of the period he wrote: 'They hit the orphanage a week ago and blew a hole in the side of the nursery, which is why the children are sheltering in the cellar. Natasha is there now. On the far side of the city, smoke is rising as straight and as black as a chimney. Something is always burning here and someone always dying. Maybe a Serb sniper is there even now, training his sights on this window. This is a city waiting to die and the world is watching. And here I sit, a stranger in Sarajevo, come to take away a little girl.'

Despite everything, many of the children were still a cheeky, chatty, friendly bunch, looking for contact and affection. Behind the bravado, the rage, the tantrums, some thoughtful and desperately sad minds were grinding away with private thoughts of their own vulnerability, a nihilism fostered by the indescribable horrors they had witnessed. Some had turned to crime and begging to get enough food and some money.

A number had been responsible for an arson attack on a disused city hotel. In what represented a childhood prank in Sarajevo, two had even cycled, in daylight, through the front lines and been captured by the Serbs. They had paraded on Serb television and were returned to the Bosnians like naughty schoolboys who could have ended up dead so easily.

I sat down with several and recorded their feelings.

Muhammed Krasnic had lost his father before the war. Then, when he was just twelve, his mother was killed in the bread queue massacre of

1992. Suddenly he was alone in the world. His first days at the orphanage were, he said, awful, filled with dread and yearning for his real home and his mother.

Afraid and vulnerable, he began to associate with older children and was still facing Bosnian court action for shoplifting and for burning down part of the city's Hotel Bristol. At fifteen, he had given up smoking and started football training. His discipline was still a problem, but he was trying to go to school and obtain better marks. For the future he was hoping to be taken in by an aunt, who was penniless because of the war and could not feed him at that time. 'My other hope is that the war will end and I can go anywhere I want,' he said.

Another of the older children who had some hope was Amin Oprasic, a former area junior boxing champion. I had brought him a donated boxing bag from England, which was strung up to a beam immediately for him to demonstrate his skills. At eighteen, he did not know why his widowed mother had sent him to the home, but he used boxing to vent his frustration and anger at his past and the war.

He was expecting to be called up for the Bosnian army, but intended to run away. He could not get over the heavy shelling which had rocked and smashed the orphanage over a year ago.

Even with eleven direct hits, the building was still in a repairable state. Outside we saw the mortar craters in the playground. We also found the mortar pits which had been dug by the Bosnian army in the grounds. In the cynical double thinking of the war's political leaders, it was no surprise to find that the home had been used as a base by the city's defenders. It was in a good tactical position from which to fire mortars. But it must have been obvious that that action would draw return fire from the Serbs. This would endanger the children and possibly ruin their only home. It would also draw condemnation of the Serbs whose bullet and shellholes would remain as a propaganda statement long after the Bosnian mortar tubes had been shepherded away.

Such publicity had made the home a 'must visit' place for media and VIPs. More than a thousand had passed through in the past three years, uttering their sympathies and pledging help. Journalists, aid workers, politicians, all had made their promises. But nothing had happened.

By the time Mark and I arrived, the director, Amir Zelic, who had run the home in the pre-war Communist days, had the stooped shoulders and ironic smile of someone who had seen it all before. He had become used to the platitudes of foreigners: 'People have come from many countries and continents, promised help, taken their pictures or film and gone away and nothing has happened.

'Many times I have felt bad because they have been picturing the children in a zoo. They have been on satellite TV and newspapers across the world, but they have had nothing.'

This time would be different. The building was a hellhole, but first reports pointed to its structural integrity being sound. Every service had been cut, from water pipes and electrical cables slashed by shrapnel, to the lights fittings and switches being stolen. But Mark was determined. Over the next few days we would be meeting a wide range of experts who had surveyed and costed the work. They would be bidding for a contract worth as much as £200,000 in a city under siege, where materials were being smuggled through the 'secret' tunnel or through the shellfire of nearby Mount Igman, the only overland route through the Serb cordon.

As we stepped outside into the home's cratered playground, Mark gave me one of those familiar determined stares, his blue eyes gleaming. He had cuddled the babies, hugged the teenagers and I knew he had been as moved as me by their plight. His words spoke volumes so I wrote them down: 'This home is more than bricks and concrete. When all the children return we must ensure that they have things to do and that they are sent to school.

'They must be encouraged and loved and looked after and not just left like they are at the moment to scavenge on the street because nobody has the time and expertise and the money – the things necessary – to give them a proper life.'

It was a vision which went beyond the construction task. It was what Mark would always stress, the human side not the institutionalised conveyor belt which many orphanages had come to represent. It seemed a distant target. But behind the charm and humour, I had come to recognise in him a streak of steely determination to succeed.

I was also determined in a professional way to defy the Serbs by beating their stranglehold on communications. A Canadian UN officer I had met had allowed me to use the satellite phone in his office to contact our people at home. The building was less than a kilometre from our apartment and stayed open late. I was able to use the link throughout the week, sending updates on our progress and short features to the newspaper which were published each day. I knew that some of the material would prove alarming for June and the children, as well as for Mark's family. But it was also spurring people on to support the massive rebuilding project with donations. On balance, that seemed worth the pain, particularly when we were also witnessing first-hand horrors which were keeping people glued to their television screens night after night at home. To make the point, it emerged that the shooting on Sniper Alley earlier had claimed the life of a little girl on a targeted tram. Her mother had also been blinded by flying glass. The French Foreign Legionnaire who had been firing the cannon from the armoured vehicle had been concussed by a sniper round which had ricocheted off his bulletproof heavy blue UN helmet. He was a brave man who had lived to tell the tale. The trams had stopped.

But they had restarted the next day.

That evening, we decided that we would go out and find one of the few restaurants still operating in the city. Fighting on the front line had dropped due to a Muslim festival, which had made the streets quieter and safer. We had been directed to a small basement place, over the river and just a few hundred metres from the Presidency, in the city centre.

Inside, we were the only guests in a candlelit room with blue and white check cloths on its dozen tables. A slightly-built waitress with black hair and matching eyes took our order for the night's only cooked offering, mutton burger and fried chipped potatoes. It would be washed down with the other offering, Sarajevo beer, a worrying concoction which we had been told had been watered down to avoid problems of drunkenness in the city during the siege. It still seemed powerful to Mark and me. After two large bottles, the food arrived at the same time as the Serbs decided it was time to rearrange the area outside. Mortar explosions began to 'walk' along the nearby streets. The windows above our heads were at street level and began to shake with the occasional ground jarring near-miss. The waitress showed her concern by closing the windows nearest to us and pulling the curtains together, smiling nervously as she left.

After a series of very close explosions, we noticed that she and a colleague from the kitchen were now under two tables in a corner. Then, as the crescendo from the streets outside became even louder, the restaurant's inner door flew open and, half-staggering, in spilled two local youths, their faces wet with cold sweat, their bodies shaking with fear. One, tall with trendily long hair and a black coat, told us in excellent English that they had never come so near to death, so close had been the pattern of mortars as they had walked along the pavement.

Mark ordered Sarajevo beers all round and the two began to recover slowly. As long coat's story unfolded, it was clear he was a streetwise seventeen-year-old man-about-town who knew every scam and had many contacts worth knowing. Behind the controlled bravado was a business brain which had seen the war interrupt his ambition to make his first million dollars before he was twenty-one. He had been charging one Deutschmark a time for car washes at city garages, paying his washing teams and the garage manager a cut and making a small fortune. Then the fuel had virtually run out and only the privileged, the taxi drivers and the local mafia were regularly driving cars.

After that blow there was no way he would die or fight willingly in this conflict. That was an option for fools.

He showed us his insurance scheme, highly professional false identity papers which purported to show he would be too young for Army service for at least another year. Immediately, Mark and I had nominated him as 'The Spiv'. He was one of those people who flourish in a war. Survivors. I half expected him to open the black coat at some point and ask if we wanted to buy wristwatches or silk stockings. Such men are always escaping from scrapes, always looking for the next opportunity, always useful to know. We described our mission and agreed to take him on as our interpreter and guide. He was a risk. But he seemed to have an affection for the orphans, some of whom he knew personally. And he appeared to regard Mark and me as trophies, rather like the trendy hair and coat. We were two amusements to show around town whilst he was at a loose end. That suited us fine.

We knew there would be difficult negotiations ahead. There was huge potential to get ripped-off. Corruption was rife, with humanitarian aid being sold and looted extensively. Even the front-line trenches on the hills overlooking the city were protected from the elements with hundreds of kilometres of the UNHCR-stamped polythene intended to repair civilians' shot-out windows. Certainly, Mark already had some expert advisers, but a new and completely independent figure interpreting and advising on the proceedings would be a very useful asset.

As the shelling outside stopped, the Spiv asked if we wanted to go to the city's trendiest open coffee bar for a coffee and a cake. We paid the bill. It was a few Deutschmarks, little to us but a fortune to the waitress. We discovered the reason for her suspicious smile. She had been captured early in the siege, gang-raped by the Serbs and returned in a prisoner exchange deal. Now she lived in Dobrinja, the heavily shelled ex-Olympic village, which meant she walked several kilometres a day to her work. That included the long stretches along Sniper Alley, in daylight.

This was a young woman, desperate for work who sometimes slept at the restaurant when the bombardments became too heavy for her to pick her way home.

Outside, the dark and rainswept streets were empty as we stepped onto the pavement of Marsala Tita avenue. The Spiv had regained his composure. His quiet friend spoke little English and appeared to have been frozen in shock, shivering occasionally.

It was then that the first cannon shell fizzed like a shooting star, from right to left, across the road ahead of us. Then two more came, followed by the heavy thuds of the Serb gunner's anti-aircraft weapon which had fired them. We stopped dead.

I had never seen anything like this before. The Spiv explained that it was common for the Serbs to fire their hillside cannon across this main junction. It disrupted life in the city centre far more dramatically than mere sniper rounds. And, sometimes, even managed to kill people.

Crossing the junction ahead would be like Russian roulette with a huge gun. The shells appeared to be solid shot, armour piercing rounds without an explosive warhead. They were white hot, flashing past at phenomenal speed, striking the road with a shriek and throwing up pieces of tarmac and rubble before bouncing off into the distance. To cross the junction would mean a frantic run of just over twenty-five metres.

In the darkness, it was probable that the gunner would not be able to see us. But if you were unlucky, one of his random shells would arrive at around head height at exactly the time you were making your sprint. The prospect of one of those heavy pieces of metal tearing through me filled me with horror. Self-preservation crossed my mind. I asked about alternative routes. But the Spiv puffed up his cheeks and shook his head, which in Sarajevo-speak meant: 'You dumb foreigner. Don't you think we would take a detour if it didn't mean more danger?'

We waited for another couple of shells to pass, then the Spiv leaned forward and shouted: 'Now!'

We were off, running for our lives, literally. I had been a reasonable sprinter in my youth, but I doubt that I ever ran as quickly. Mark was alongside me, together with the quiet one, his face still white, now creased with fear lines. The short run felt like an eternity. I couldn't help considering its implications as I took a deep breath, held it, lifted myself onto my toes, punched hard and began sprinting. The situation reminded me of that day when I was a convent boy in short trousers and a teenage bully with a metal catapult loaded with a heavy steel ball, had forced me to run with two friends across a narrow valley. 'I'll give you five seconds before I fire,' he had warned. We stumbled down the slope like frenzied gazelles, before struggling hard, in a line, up the other side. We were almost level with him when he fired. I heard the 'thwack' of the released heavy rubber and the 'fizz' of the metal ball slicing through the air toward us. Then there was the awful 'wumpf' of the ball as it struck the back of the head of the boy on my right, stopping us dead, leaving him bleeding and us crying.

It is strange how such childhood memories bubble to the surface at times of great stress and trauma. But on a darkened street in Sarajevo, this was one of them.

As we came out of the cover of the buildings, my peripheral vision picked out the side street and the ominous dark bulk of the hill to our right, framed against a now-starry sky. It was there that a man was perched, probably drunk at that time of night, looking through the sights of his fearsome cannon and punching out shells with careless disregard for logic, humanity or any apparent routine. If he fired now I knew I would see the gunflash first. I had not fully worked it out at the time, but it is disheartening to know that the bright glow would be the first element in the sequence to reach my retina, its light travelling at just under 300 million metres a second. Next would be that heavy white cylinder of metal, moving at around 7,500 metres per second. It would strike with the force of an express train. I had already seen what such heavy weapons could do to the human body. It would tear part or all of me to pieces, as the violence of its impact velocity and residual kinetic energy threw me many metres across the road. Next, and almost incidentally, would come the sound of the blast, reaching my ears at a tortoise-like 340 metres a second. That was the part which normally made people duck instinctively. Far too late.

Such are the mind's machinations when facing terror of this nature. As I strained to bring my legs into the next stride as quickly as my body would allow me, I seemed to have time to wonder, too, what the others were thinking as we were linked in this race against death.

Then we were safe, across the junction, sheltered by the row of shops and offices that ran the length of the road. As we gathered our breath, we laughed with the excitement of survival and started walking again. A few seconds later came a flash and a thud behind us. It was the next cannon shell coming in. It had been a tight squeeze. My heart was pounding like a hammer in my head. I put it down to adrenalin. But it was probably fear.

The next few days became a near-surreal round of conflicting images. At times it was difficult to imagine the scenes were not just some bad dream. In a variety of homes and offices, we found ourselves negotiating written estimates for the orphanage contract with building companies which were still able to function despite the war. Their bids varied widely. Our problem was knowing which company would be the optimum choice: able to achieve the rebuilding work at a cost that was reasonable and assured a good quality result.

In one city centre office block, we were shown up to the third floor to a comfortable suite complete with deep windows and well-kept rubber plants. At that altitude and with so much glass, it was not difficult to look across to the Serb positions to the south and east. Sniping regularly punctuated the meeting at which the contracting manager gave a detailed assessment of his plans for manpower and materials. I found myself developing an embarrassing flinch each time a bullet hissed past those huge windows. I was the only one flinching round that heavy table. Concentration was difficult in the circumstances.

But it was during a few particularly close rounds of firing when we were talking about the smuggling of Italian lamps and glazing through the tunnel that I felt a distinct urge to duck under the comforting polished thick wood.

Street sign, Sarajevo 1994

Mandy O'Toole hands over her BUPA teddy bear, Sarajevo 1994

The Spiv, Sarajevo 1995

Rapid Reaction Force base, Ploce 1995

After the storm, Ploce 1995

The Bosnia Toy Appeal, Norwich 1996

Instead, as I simply feigned concentration on the matters under discussion, something prevented me from making a complete fool of myself. It may have been the contractor's young and elegantly dressed secretary, placing coffee cups in front of us with precision and a steady hand. It may have been that British composure which is part of our psyche. I dismissed thoughts of the adage: 'Better to be a live coward than a dead hero.' There were standards to uphold here. So I drank my coffee slowly and sank as low in my seat as possible, without looking like I was taking cover.

It was later that Mark joked about some of the exaggerated precautions I appeared to be taking. He had noticed something in particular. Whenever we were on streets observed lengthways by the sniper positions, 'enfiladed' is the military description, I had started walking as close to the adjoining walls as possible, providing a slightly more difficult target.

This was not an embarrassing display of knee-knocking cowardice, or so I convinced myself. It was behaviour prompted simply by a subliminal concern for my safety. I wanted to give myself the best chance possible of going home balanced against the risks required to get the job done.

On the surface, we were becoming more used to the gunfire, running when the Sarajevans ran, hiding when they hid. Mostly we were beginning to act instinctively, trying to compartmentalise the war so that we could concentrate with clarity on the crucial contract.

But somewhere in my subconscious were those warnings from the MSF security team on my previous trip. I was breaking almost every rule in their book: walking the streets without a helmet or personal radio, in a bright blue waterproof and with just a hope that the statistics were on my side. It was a deep-seated mixture of guilt and fear which made me take those precautions: guilt at exposing my children to a life without their father; fear that I might be one of the unlucky ones.

As the week went on, talks were held with the developing project team, people Mark felt he could trust: the lawyer, banker and architect who would ensure the chosen construction company kept to its agreed standards and timetable. Sarajevo City Council agreed to oversee the rebuilding work and Lady Chalker came up trumps again by offering help from her skilled and versatile engineering team.

Another supporter was young and bespectacled Robert Barnett, Britain's first ambassador to Bosnia. Norfolk-educated, his parents still lived on the coast at the pretty fishing resort of Wells-next-the-Sea and he had great affection for his home county and the *Eastern Daily Press*. Consequently, he was also determined to do what he could to support the project. At that time, British foreign policy over the war was in a terrible muddle. London appeared to be attempting to maintain its linkage with the Serbs in Belgrade at the expense of its relations with the embattled government of Bosnian President Izetbegovic in Sarajevo. It was a fudge which was viewed by ordinary Sarajevans as duplicity. Most had given up hope of salvation coming from what many saw as the double-crossing, weakly-led governments of Europe. They talked instead of 'the coming of Uncle Sam'. Whilst many British politicians had excused their lack of action against the Serbs with dire warnings about the Muslim threat posed to Europe by an independent Bosnia, the Americans had been largely united in their condemnation of Serb atrocities and the need for a forceful military and political strategy. At a time when the United Nations special envoy Yasushi Akashi was warning that ceasefires were breaking down and the war was escalating again, the streets of Bosnia's capital were alive with calls for American air power to sweep the Serbs from their hills. The time was drawing closer.

Despite swimming in such muddy diplomatic waters, Britain's Ambassador was completely single-minded in his support of the Bosnian cause. It had been on a visit to Sarajevo with Lady Chalker that he had suggested the setting-up of a British embassy. 'Yes,' she had replied. 'Good idea. Why don't you become the first ambassador?'

Over the ensuing twelve months, this cultured and sharp-minded, forty-year-old career diplomat had been horrified at the cruelty he had seen meted out by the Serbs on innocent Bosnian civilians. He had steered funds into rebuilding projects in schools and now the orphanage. As I walked with him through the city, I was staggered at the friendliness shown to him by ordinary Sarajevans, who passed and offered greetings. One young woman broadcaster from the city summed up the view: 'We hate your government for what it has failed to do, but we love your ambassador for what he has done for us.'

That week happened to be his last in Sarajevo. He was going home to his family at the end of a tumultuous year in office. Even so, he expended a great deal of time and effort on Mark and me. I was greatly impressed at seeing the art of the diplomat in action. In a restaurant, he would introduce us to key UN and other people who were to become very useful contacts. In the bathroom of his small flat above a sock factory, I saw how he had washed and shaved every morning under the watchful eye of the snipers on one of the city's most dangerous hills. We had laughed at the ignominy of being sniped whilst covered in shaving cream. He had also shown me a little of the cynicism of this city at war. Adjoining the sock factory, we peered through the window of a small building where a roulette wheel was spinning. This was Sarajevo's casino, which had operated throughout the war for the benefit of the arms dealers, the mafia and the profiteers. Greed and corruption were still alive and well in this city of the dead.

Before he left he also took me to the Isak Samokovliska junior school, one of those particularly tragic examples of youthful innocence being crushed by the cruelty of adults. Just 200 metres from Sniper Alley, the school had taken unspeakable punishment throughout the siege. Robert Barnett had taken it to his heart, using his influence to help rebuild its shattered fabric each time a Serb gunner decided it was time to turn his attentions on its children. On the day of his farewell, snipers shot out some of the newly-glazed upstairs windows. Some of their bullets hammered into the walls of classrooms alongside children's paintings of trees and fields. Bullets from adults. Paintings from children. The resonance of this montage was not lost on any of us who attended the farewell party.

As the youngsters sang, danced and performed a drama in the ambassador's honour, there was a feeling of true warmth and not the stage-managed soulless affair which such occasions can become. It was hard not to cry when a tiny, pale-faced girl in a green headband, stepped forward and declared in heavily accented English: 'Mr Barnett, you are part of our school and you will forever be in our hearts.'

As we strolled through the city streets later, he told me of his passion to continue helping the school, even after he had left. With that steely look and quiet voice, he turned to me and said: 'The contact will go on. There are some pieces of unfinished work I must do.'

And you knew he meant it.

Despite such diversions, Mark and I were continuing our round of talks with construction companies and spending as much time as possible with the orphans. Their names and faces were beginning to have real meaning as individuals. I was taking dozens of pictures of them and filing stories on the UN satellite link every evening. One such story epitomised the children's suffering. It involved Amir Agic, a two-year-old who spent most of his time swaying in his cot in the baby room, where he was fed, bathed and had his nappy changed regularly but could hardly have the love he craved with so few staff among so many youngsters. His black eyes were huge discs in a round face beneath a shock of black curly hair.

He had arrived at the home after his mother was imprisoned for killing his drunken father with an axe. The father had just launched another vicious assault on the mother's already battered and pregnant body and she had cracked. She was facing many years in prison. Little Amir was facing a life without the warm embrace of a loving parent. He was oblivious to the cruel hand which fate had dealt him and unconcerned by the crump of artillery and crack of bullets which were the daily cacophony of his awful world.

Somehow the young seemed to cope better than adults with the horrors around them. I saw that mirrored in the wide and despairing eyes of Dina Dulic, a nurse at the Kosevo Hospital whom I had promised to visit. We had become friends on the previous trip with the surgical team.

In the past fourteen months all her close colleagues had gone. Some had been caught by the snipers on that deadly walk to work. Most had made their long-planned escapes to join relatives in far-flung parts of the world. She had given me her precious coffee, her jokes and her affection on my last visit. This time she was close to tears, the despair carved across her unsmiling face as she told of her fears for her young family and for her own future. She greeted me with a hug and tears in her eyes on the hospital's third floor plastic surgery unit. My gifts of chocolates, cosmetics and medical equipment brought more tears and words of affection for the 'fun team' of which I had been a part.

'Tell them all I think of them all the time,' she murmured. 'They brought so much light into our lives. Sometimes I meet the people they operated on. I must have seen thirty of them, walking in the streets. They are all so grateful and they ask me if I have heard from you.'

Her face had beamed momentarily at the memory of that time. Then she clouded over again.

'It seems a lifetime away. So much hope, so much joy has gone since then. All this hatred, all this killing, it is too much to bear, too long and too much ...'

Her voice tailed off and we hugged again. And we cried together. Her tears were tears of despair and fear. Mine were tears of frustration and anger and pity. I knew I would have to leave this young woman soon who was so kind and had devoted her life to nursing the sick. She had no relatives abroad to claim her, no money to bribe her way through checkpoints or tunnels. She was trapped with her family, until peace or death ended her limbo. My heart went out to her as I left.

That night, Mark and I discussed the contract tenders in fine detail, together with the arrangements for financing and administering the project. Head and shoulders above the rest was a bid made by a young architect, Vesna, and her highly skilled joiner husband Osman. Her quotation was moderate. But her enthusiasm, compassion for the children and apparent sincerity won us over. Vesna was to become a superb choice in the final analysis. But at that point we knew her and Osman as the struggling parents of two polite teenage boys who had all fled when the Serbs took over their home in the suburb of Illidza. They had lived comfortably in a home, lovingly created by Osman with countless features carved and assembled from fine woods, which could now be seen only in the pictures they had taken before they left. Their savings, they told us, had been buried under a rose tree in the front garden, ready for their return. But for a Bosnian Muslim couple like them, to go back there then would have meant almost certain death.

In the meantime, they had been taken in by relatives in the city. But there had been no work for architects or joiners and they had used their entrepreneurial skills to open a small rented shop in the city centre, selling the oils and watercolours of artist friends to politicians, journalists and anyone else who still had hard currency. Vesna had shown us where they had lived for months like rats, sleeping on trestles in a windowless store-room at the back of the shop when the shelling at their relatives' apartment had torn off part of the roof.

'I wanted to keep my boys alive,' this elegant and determined woman told me, with complete simplicity.

We knew this would be their first major project since their escape. But, somehow, they appeared right: honest, skilled and with a thirst to succeed, unlike some of the slicker contractors we had interviewed.

With the deal agreed, Mark and I settled back in our apartment to polish off too much of the duty-free Glenmorangie which we had promised ourselves for a celebration. It was freezing in the unheated bedroom, where we shivered in thick sweaters. That night we enjoyed the warmth that comes from reaching a good decision, supported by large glasses of some of Scotland's finest malt.

Next morning I was still feeling that warmth as I announced to Mark that I had had an outrageous idea: why don't I stroll down the road and ask the President for a personal interview about the orphanage project? It was not quite the madcap proposal it seemed: our talks had included meetings with the city council and, in the inter-related way of most things in the city, the President's brother just happened to be heading the section which would oversee the rebuilding work. We had already been told by leading officials that this was the biggest single such project to have been launched in the city since the siege had begun.

So we were in the big league, symbolically and politically, from their viewpoint. They wanted foreign investment and reconstruction to start, not just humanitarian aid. It signified their intention to keep Sarajevo for Bosnia, despite the Serb efforts to eject them.

Mark seemed sceptical about my mission. 'Do you really think it will be that simple to get an audience with Itzy?' he asked incredulously.

I shrugged: 'Who knows? I once met a Turkish journalist who reckoned all you had to do was to bluff your way in with persistence and you could see virtually anyone. He had interviewed Yeltsin and Clinton and was aiming to try the system on John Major next.'

So off I went, fired up by heavy optimism to try for an interview with one of the world's best protected – and most targeted – political leaders.

The Presidency was a little over a kilometre away, a relatively easy walk through several side streets and across a road bridge. We had passed its gaunt, unimpressive exterior many times, noting where the Serbs had slammed numerous cannon shells into its walls and gardens.

It was when I came to the bridge that my optimism melted away. It was a crude feature with steel arches, completely exposed to the forested hills behind me. Somewhat bemused, I was already on its approach road when I noticed the few people ahead of me were running. I heard the familiar crack of a sniper's overshoot. Then another and another. Two old men were huddled inside the bridge arches, pointing at the hills and shouting something in Bosnian.

I ran toward the bridge. It immediately occurred to me that I should have been running the much shorter distance back to cover. But my guard had, for once, been down. The green bulletproof jacket began to weigh heavily and chafe at my neck as I strained for more speed. I passed the two old men, one with a beret, his mouth open, shouting unknown words. The other, his head covered by a black balaclava, flinching behind the narrow grey steel girders, looked grimly at me.

To my left I passed another figure, a woman in a long navy blue coat, lying in the roadway, face down, but groaning pitifully.

I did not stop. Nor did the three figures in front of me, who were heading for the cover of the street corner. I imagined I heard more cracks, even several metallic clinks of near-misses on the roadway to my right. But the adrenalin was playing havoc with my senses. All I could think was what a tempting target my blue jacket must have seemed to the men on the hill, peering through their scopes at the tiny figures on the bridge.

As I skidded into the shelter of the buildings, I collided with another of the runners, whom I had caught up with, knocking both of us to the floor. A middle-aged man with grey hair and padded green coat, he grunted something at me. It seemed like an oath. But it may have been a warning. Then he jumped up and made off.

I joined him, running down the street, realising that we were still exposed there to snipers on an adjoining hillside.

Neither of us was sparing a thought for the wounded woman on the bridge. That was the way of Sarajevo. Too many had been lured to their deaths trying to help the fallen. The snipers wounded people deliberately as a trap for the compassionate. Everyone knew that.

It was only when I arrived at the Presidency square that I stopped running and dived into a doorway to catch my breath and some sense of balance. I extracted from my heavy canvas Samsonite bag everything I would need to penetrate the security cordon. Press card, passport and my well battered 35 millimetre Nikon, with an impressive zoom lens and gigantic flash unit.

As I approached the entrance, I announced myself to the two soldiers huddled behind their sandbags.

'James Ruddy, British journalist, here to see the President for an interview,' I declared without much conviction.

They looked stunned, checked my documents and frisked me as I kept talking about being a little early, but hoping to get in out of the rain.

And it worked. They told me to report to a secretary on the first floor. And in I went. Up the small staircase along a corridor and into a large anteroom where a well-dressed young man asked me, in beautifully crisp English, what I required. I figured he had been pre-warned about my arrival by the soldiers. I said I was here to interview the President about the orphanage project if at all possible.

Far from receiving an immediate negative response, I was invited to take a seat and he would check with his superior. I figured this was old-style Communist collective responsibility in progress. Not so much courtesy, more about passing the buck. And so it went on, for at least an hour, as a variety of officials emerged to establish the credentials and intentions of the strange Brit in the anteroom.

Eventually, a sophisticated young man in a well-pressed blue suit emerged and advised me that the President was not in today, but could I come back in two days at 11 o'clock.

Sadly, I was intending to leave the next day and had to decline. Slick blue suit looked disappointed. He clearly felt there was a publicity opportunity going begging and suggested I wait for him to see if he could get somebody else. I had had enough of meetings with political placemen throughout the week and stepped out into the corridor as soon as he left.

As I was heading for the stairs, a woman poked her head out of an office door and spoke to me in Bosnian.

'Sorry,' I said, 'I'm a British journalist and don't speak your language.'

'Never mind, come in anyway, and have some cake. We are celebrating,' she said in perfect English.

I found myself in a room with leading members of the education ministry enjoying hot tea and the first cake I had tasted for more than a week. It was a thick, fruity affair, the kind my mother used to call slab cake, and it tasted like heaven after so many dried meals and muttonburgers.

The two women and a man were fascinated when I told them of my mission to meet the President. They knew of the orphanage project and spoke in admiring tones about Mark's courage and dedication. They did not seem to have heard of me. But they were too cultured to allow that to spoil our meeting. After the events on the bridge, this was a wonderful respite. I was angry with myself when they confirmed that the President would most probably have been delighted to have given me an interview if I had caught up with him. As a journalist this would have been something of a scoop which would have added major gravitas to our mission. The story of the President's support for the orphanage project would have been followed up by the rest of the story-hungry media. Everyone knew it would also have been a propaganda coup for the Bosnian's reconstruction aims. But then it was always difficult to divide propaganda from objective news.

As I stepped out through the front door again, I realised it was the same doorway which had recently featured on the BBC television news. The footage had shown the arrival of the President and a major delegation, followed by Serb cannon shells punching their way into the concrete lintels in apparent slow motion. There had been no explosions, indicating the rounds were solid shot and intended to humiliate rather than maim any of the visiting leaders.

The memory confirmed again how vulnerable we all were. It was probably due to the Glenmorangie, but I had an immediate vision of a shoal of goldfish in a glass bowl being pebble-bombed by a naughty boy whose mother was nowhere to be seen.

Later I had arranged to meet up with the Spiv at a local cafe. Mark and I had employed him successfully through the week and I intended to pay him for his trouble. His cunning and language skills had been invaluable. On occasions, he had even advised us not to trust some of the people we had encountered, providing a rundown on their backgrounds. He had even pulled out the huge ·357 magnum revolver which he always carried in an inside pocket, offering me, with some apology, a mere ·45 automatic for my own protection.

He was baffled when I declined and warned me that almost every young person carried a gun in the city and there were regular shootings in the cafes and clubs. I had asked him if he had used the magnum and he had answered sparingly, with another of those looks of bafflement: 'Of course.'

That afternoon the Spiv showed me one place where even he warned that he could not protect me: the central marketplace. Journalists were not welcome there, he told me. So I was not to take any pictures or ask any questions.

It was here, thirteen months earlier, that the city's worst atrocity had happened.

On 5 February 1994, at 12.37pm, a single mortar bomb had hurtled out of a sunny, spring sky into the busy city centre collection of stalls, in the shadow of the catholic cathedral. Sixty-nine people died and more than two hundred were wounded. The scale of the massacre had been due to the shopping area being packed on a pleasant day which had been relatively peaceful. Some witnesses said the effects of the bomb had been worsened because it had struck an overhead plastic canopy and exploded just above head height. The resulting blast had been an air burst, creating a huge overhead shock wave accompanied by thousands of shards of deadly hot shrapnel that tore into the unprotected shoppers and stallholders.

Worldwide condemnation and revulsion followed immediately. Yet there were the usual denials of responsibility by the Bosnian Serb leader Radovan Karadzic. These always occurred when there was a single major loss of life caused by the indiscriminate Serb shelling of the city's streets. In a familiar tactic, he accused the Bosnians of firing the round into their own people, as a means to encourage greater Nato military support for their cause. It was significant that he seldom found the need to make such pronouncements on the less spectacular days when his snipers and mortar crews were picking off civilians in ones and twos. Almost 10,000 people, many of them children, were lying in the sprawling sportsfield cemetery created near the Zetra stadium. Karadzic had found no excuses for their deaths. Every few metres along virtually every street in the city centre, you could find the familiar 'Sarajevo rose' impact points, where the Serbs had 'walked' their mortar bombs along the roads and pavements.

The truth about the market atrocity was elusive. UN military experts' findings were inconclusive. They checked out the impact and found it had come from the north-east, where both sides had mortar positions. In actuality, though, the mortar could never have been predicted to have caused such mayhem. Many Sarajevans would tell you stories about spies and fifth columnists who were aiding the Serbs. A favourite story was of the young woman artist who had been seen drawing cartographically-accurate pictures of key areas where civilians would mass. Such theories supported the accurate mortar bombing of a water queue inside a covered building and the regular pinpoint mortaring of the meeting point of a five-street junction near the orphanage. When placed in the appropriate spot, shrapnel from such single impacts had often killed and injured many people walking along all five adjoining streets.

Such stories were an understandable manifestation of the paranoia and suspicion thrown up by all wars against civilians. It seemed more likely that the market place massacre had been caused by one of those many thousands of hopeful mortar shots aimed with careless ease into the city centre by the Serb psycopaths in the surrounding hills.

It was grey and forbidding when we walked the aisles between its polythene-covered stalls. I bought three small oranges and wondered at the thoughts of the scores of people who were milling around once again. Did they think of those who died? Did they wonder if the Serbs would try to repeat the event?

With practised subterfuge, the Spiv indicated with his foot the Sarajevo rose which marked where the single bomb had finally splattered against one of the concrete walkways between the stalls. I felt uncomfortable, almost a voyeur. This place had a feel of searing tragedy caused by untold evil. Hatred appeared just below the surface of those present. Time had passed, but it had not healed the anger which you could touch. It felt as if the production of a camera there would result in the owner being torn limb from limb. Even the Spiv, who had confronted danger head-on throughout the siege, decided we should go quickly.

'This place is not safe for you,' he whispered. 'They sense you. It is a feeling about you. They are talking. Something will happen if we do not go. Come now.'

With that, he had grabbed me and we were moving with speed down the wet pavement, away from that place of brooding malevolence, where the voices of dying had been replaced by the vengeful whispers of their friends and relatives.

Next morning I was due to leave Sarajevo alone. Mark was staying on to complete further business at the home. We exchanged our usual disparaging farewells as I headed for a taxi I was to share with a veteran of Sarajevo, Nigel Osborne, music professor at Edinburgh University. A tall middle-aged bearded figure, carrying a rucksack topped off with his trademark Second World War British Tommy steel helmet, he had made many trips into the capital to help his Bosnian friends.

Among his recent achievements had been the production of a complete opera in the city in just two weeks, an accomplishment which received worldwide media coverage. It was thought that he was on a Serb death list because of his active opposition to their war aims. The Bosnian Government held him in such high esteem that he had become the only non-Bosnian to have been allowed to enter or leave the city through the 'secret' airport tunnel.

This time we would be the only passengers on an otherwise empty Canadian C-130 transport plane, if we managed to get off. There were concerns that 'Maybe Airlines' would not be running that day because of some recent problems. Among them, a UN flight the previous day from Zagreb had turned back with five bullet holes in the fuselage, leading to the cancellation of all flights.

Our taxi was to take us to the UN's base at the fortified PTT building where we would be picked up by an approved and hopefully armoured vehicle to pass through the front lines to the airport. But, to my chagrin, the driver appeared confused about the safest route that day. As we neared the building's perimeter, the car slammed to a halt near a guard post where a Bosnian soldier was sheltering. We were directly in line of fire from a line of ugly grey flats on the Serb side of the river. Our driver looked terrified and began shouting. The soldier was also shouting. I ducked as low as I could in the rear seat. Nigel stepped out and walked toward the soldier, returning leisurely, his helmet jiggling on his rucksack as he walked.

'What was he shouting about?' I asked.

'He says there are many snipers here today and that we must go back.'

Nigel translated for the blubbering driver. But he refused to go the approved way, gunning the car instead on what seemed like a highly exposed route to our pick-up point. I was beginning to wonder what it was about Sarajevo taxis that made them so unpredictable. I came to the conclusion that it was probably connected with money. You could go the dangerous way cheaply or the safe way for a sizeable fee. The secret was to negotiate in advance.

When the man dropped us off, Nigel bade him farewell in fluent Bosnian with due courtesy, then struck up a conversation in fluent French with the two Foreign Legionnaires on the PTT guard post.

That day the flights were going out, much to my relief. At the airport, when our plane arrived, its engines never stopped, as it was unloaded with the speed and efficiency of a Formula One pit crew. Inside it was a vision of military precision, completely empty apart from the two of us and the green helmeted loadmaster. It was also spotless, smelling only faintly of grease, oil and high octane aviation fuel.

The Canadians, like the Brits, were proponents of the Khe Sanh dive and take-off. Within seconds of strapping in to the jump seats, we were heading for a full power, high angle climb into the cloudless sky. With around a dozen flights in and out per day at that time, there was a fair chance you would be lucky in this lottery of life and death. The Bosnian Serb gunners alongside the runway either held their fire or missed the big green bird.

When we touched down later at Italy's Ancona airport, we stepped off the rear loading ramp and received a warm greeting from a smiling young RAF flightmaster.

Nearby we could see the huge Russian-built armoured Illyushin aid aircraft whose commercial operators were refusing to make any more trips after it had been hit by ground fire on more than twenty separate occasions, the last resulting in bullets tearing through the cockpit and narrowly missing the crew.

Perhaps, I thought, they ought to start considering the Khe Sanh manoeuvre instead of their ground-hugging sorties. I decided against suggesting it to them.

Ancona had been chosen by the UN, along with Zagreb and Split, as a major staging base for its mercy airlift to Sarajevo. The industrial resort port was certainly not picked for the charm of its scenery or the attractions of its architecture. Even so, I felt like I was stepping back into another world again.

In the taxi into town, Nigel impressed me once more with his linguistic skills, this time discussing food with the driver in fluent Italian.

It was a few hours later, whilst enjoying our first proper meal in a long time in the Ancona Railway Station restaurant, that I agreed to take part in one of Nigel's plots to deliver a major cultural blow on behalf of the oppressed people of his beloved Bosnia …

INTERLUDE

A CONCERT

It seemed an idea that was doomed from the start.
But then you could have said the same about most of what I had been involved with in recent years.

I was perched on a cafe stool in the heart of unattractive Ancona, mulling over my rather rash agreement to Nigel Osborne's grand plan.

And the more I thought through the details, the more it seemed totally hopeless.

The professor was a whirlwind of thoughts and actions. He had grown to love Bosnia and Sarajevo before the war, walking its hills and mountains, admiring its tolerance and rich cultural mix. He had braved the siege many times, sometimes sneaking into the city at extraordinary risk to his life. His aim was to foster that culture, particularly its music. His recent opera there had been an unabashed exploration of its suffering.

Now he was to go a step further.

His aim was to arrange for the airlift of the Sarajevo String Quartet to Britain for a series of concerts highlighting the city's suffering and raising much-needed funding. They would be the first Sarajevans to be allowed out of the capital by the Serbs on a UN flight.

Over our freshly-made minestrone and huge platefuls of Italian mixed meat and pasta salad, washed down by a carafe of local rosé at the railway station restaurant earlier in the day, he had tried to convince me of the viability of his scheme. The negotiations were under way. The chances of success were very good.

And, if the plan was successful, the quartet would be out in just over two weeks, starting a concert tour of British cathedrals.

Norwich, he had observed, had a cathedral. Not only that, he had developed close links with the University of East Anglia, on the edge of the city, by supporting its efforts to rebuild Sarajevo's music library.

'So James,' he said with the look of a poker player who has just laid down a winning hand, 'what do you think?'

It may have been the rosé affecting my powers of reasoning, but I played for time: 'What do I think about what Nigel?'

'About organising a concert in Norwich?' he replied.

I had great difficulty in swallowing the next mouthful of pasta. When I did, I reached for a napkin, wiped the sauce from my lips and uttered a stream of doubts.

'What! The cathedral holds hundreds of people. I've never organised a concert in my life. We've only got a couple of weeks. And – and this is a big *and* – we don't even know if the musicians are going to be let out.'

Already, though, I was beginning to waver. Before Nigel started his soothing soliloquy of reassuring noises, I was convinced this exercise was worth risking the prospect of a complete foul-up. After seeing the horrors and joys of the past week, I was angry: angry at the media manipulation which was being conducted by both sides in Sarajevo. But, like the professor of music sitting opposite, I was mostly angry at the genocidal Serbs who were being allowed to massacre so many innocents, and angry at the governments of Britain and Europe for allowing it to happen.

I was also acutely aware that the people of East Anglia, who had done so much to help our missions, deserved the chance to feel the kind of emotion the quartet could generate. The performance I had witnessed the previous year had moved many people to tears.

'Alright, Nigel,' I promised, 'put Norwich on your British tour list. I may live to regret this.'

Smiling broadly, he raised his glass, clinked the bowl against mine and toasted our agreement with a chuckle.

Then he was off. With a firm handshake, the tall figure was heading for the Bologna train, muttering something about seeing friends there, waving energetically, his tin helmet bouncing on that old green rucksack.

I was alone again in a strange town. It was an odd feeling. I had my first hot shower at the Hotel Rosa, a small budget place across the road from the station. Like the hot food, it was one of those treats which I had savoured in my dreams in that freezing apartment.

That evening I rang home, phoned a story to the office and then made a listless and lonely tour of the centre of Ancona.

I had checked in my bulletproof jacket at the airport and it seemed strange to walk the streets without it. I found myself hesitating at junctions, looking for snipers as well as oncoming cars. It reminded me of that time in Southern Croatia when photographer Simon Finlay and I were making our first trip into the war. We were walking the quiet Roman alleys on the peaceful island of Krk when two boys had thrown 'Jumping Jack' fireworks into our path. Both of us had dived for cover, our nerves jangling, hearts thumping. Then we had been left feeling faintly ridiculous as the boys laughed at their successful jape.

What, I wondered, would it be like for the string quartet to come to England after years, not just a few days, of living with death.

Next day, flying home, I had plenty of time to plan. I was always keen on a detailed hit list and drew up a comprehensive agenda which would give the concert a chance of success, however slim.

It did not escape me that the date fixed for the event was April Fool's day.

By the middle of March, I had produced publicity material, printed tickets, written pieces for the newspaper and spread the word about the concert as far and wide as possible.

The cathedral officials had been very accommodating, providing me with the 900-year-old Norman edifice free of charge, along with security, changing facilities and whatever sound equipment I needed.

With just two weeks to go, the quartet still did not have permission to fly out. Nigel was comforting in every phone call, soothing my concerns like someone who had handled such chaos many times before.

By March 24th, there was continuing shelling and sniping in Sarajevo, despite the four-month ceasefire negotiated by ex-US President Jimmy Carter the previous December. All sides had used this lull to build up forces for a spring offensive. The Bosnian army was also holding out against concerted Serb attacks on the so-called UN safe area of Bihac. For what it mattered, it was also admitted at this time by the UN that it did not record deaths from ceasefire violations unless there was evidence that the sniper belonged to a particular faction and the victim to another. Some chance, I thought.

I was becoming increasingly pessimistic and was forced to alert people to the likelihood that the concert might be off, despite my early optimism. I had to admit to the obvious in a newspaper announcement: 'The British Embassy (in Sarajevo) is backing our efforts to get the musicians out, but the military situation is closing in.'

Then, two days later, the Serbs relented and allowed the musicians out onto an aid flight to Zagreb during a lull in the fighting. Nigel rang me and was ecstatic: 'There is just one problem, James, they are missing their cellist.'

So, we had a concert, but just a trio to play as a quartet. If this was show-business, I thought, give me journalism any time.

The cellist, it was reported, had been so relieved to have escaped alive from Sarajevo, that he was refusing to go back when the time came. That had given the authorities problems with issuing him the necessary visas when the plane arrived in Zagreb. In effect, he was claiming refugee status and would be remaining in the Croatian capital. It seemed a some-what dramatic decision, but who could blame him for wanting to give himself the chance of a proper life? Thousands of others had escaped, but not in such a widely publicised manner. I wondered what his fellow musicians thought of his decision. Sarajevans can be particularly judgemental and opinionated, which is one of the city's attractive idiosyncrasies.

Even so, I should not have doubted Nigel's resourcefulness in the face of such a problem. By the time the party had arrived at Heathrow he had already arranged for a British musician to take the missing man's place. They arrived at Hazelwood House, Devon, just a few hours before their first concert there and held a short rehearsal. The programme was to be a selection of well-known works of Dvorak, Haydn, Schubert, Grieg and, their *pièce de résistance*, Albinoni's Adagio.

It was all systems go for the Norwich concert, set for just a couple of days later and I plugged it unashamedly everywhere I could.

That night I awoke after a dream in which I was standing in the cathedral, introducing the musicians and staring at empty seats with the great wooden doors banging in the wind at the rear of the huge nave. It was my worst nightmare.

As it happened, almost 400 people turned up and appeared deeply .moved by the event. On the personal address system, I told them how the musicians had braved the city's deadly streets for so long, travelling to and from rehearsals and concerts, keeping their culture alive. The membership of the group had changed in that time, as some had paid the ultimate price for their courage. Others had simply escaped overseas, unable to face the grinding depression any longer.

When they played, I could sense something unusual in the air. This was a time when British television news was filled with nightly footage of the dead and the dying of Sarajevo in particular. The audience was peculiarly quiet, respectful, displaying empathy with the group's suffering.

It was a feeling which several people mentioned to me later: a unique linking of players and listeners in a common bond.

The only instances of lightness came from the guest star Nigel Blomiley, of the BBC Concert Orchestra, who had agreed to stand in for the missing musician. Nigel was a lively and extrovert performer whose characteristic warmth and pleasure in his art was instantly magnetic. He was so moved by the event that he offered himself, without a fee, for the rest of the tour. But even he was upstaged just before the interval by an unexpected addition to the party. Viola player, Dijana Ihas had managed to convince the Serbs that she needed to bring her baby on the extraordinary expedition because she was breast-feeding him. As feeding time was approaching, he bellowed loudly from the sacristy, his healthy lungs producing a resonance that echoed throughout those ancient cathedral walls. It was as if a tiny child of tortured Bosnia was enjoying his freedom in the only way he knew.

That evening I took the musicians to an Indian restaurant where they enjoyed the delights of a British traditional night out. To underline the cultural nature of the experience, they were also treated to a strippagram, arranged for the birthday boy on an adjoining tableful of rugby players. My modest powers of translation deserted me when these cultured and serious academics inquired enthusiastically why a woman in a maid's uniform had stepped into the room and was removing her clothes.

It was, I thought, better left to their imagination.

They departed the next day on another stage of the whistlestop tour, tired and elated, but also grateful for the hospitality and kindness the people of Norfolk had shown them, however brief their stay.

I was relieved that the concert had been a success. It had given a few hundred people a taste of the raw emotion which I had experienced from witnessing the tragedy of Sarajevo. Television pictures could never convey that message as movingly as these three talented musicians, a British maestro and a small baby.

It had been a privilege to have been involved. As I waved them off, I wondered at their courage at returning to their home of so much sorrow.

FIRST UK CONCERT TOUR BY

SARAJEVO STRING QUARTET

NORWICH CATHEDRAL
SATURDAY, APRIL 1ST, 7.30PM

IN AID OF THE CHILDREN OF SARAJEVO'S LJUBICE IVEZIC
ORPHANAGE

SUPPORTED BY THE EASTERN DAILY PRESS

Saturday April 1st 1995 7.30pm
Norwich Cathedral

Programme

Dzevad Sabanagic	*Violin*
Igor Simonji	*Violin*
Dijana Ihas	*Viola*
and	
Nigel Blomiley	*Cello*

Mozart	Divertimento No 3 Allegro
A Dvorak	Lento from Quartet op 96 in F Sharp
L Boccherini	Menueto
Haydn	Serenade
Albinoni	Adagio
Mozart	Eine Kleine Nachtmusik
David Wilde	Prayer for Bosnia

Interval

PI Tschaikovski	Andante Cantabile
Schubert	String Quartet in D minor "Death and the Maiden"

Fin

87

History and profiles

The Sarajevo String Quartet is based at the Chamber Theatre 55 in Sarajevo. Its members have played over 200 concerts since the start of the siege of the city three years ago. This has brought music to the ears of people wherever they have still been able to gather, including bombed-out front line houses where the city's defenders have gathered as a brief respite from the war. The musicians have also braved regular shelling and sniping to take part in many hundreds of rehearsals in their dedicated pursuit of their art. As a group, they have made records for the radio and television of Bosnia and Herzegovina. A stunning documentary has also been made by Vefik Hadzismajlovic of their work and performances through the horrors of the war.

> *"Their powerful spiritual weapon presents a way of hope to a better tomorrow and a creative fortress against an unavoidable future..."*
>
> **Gradimir Gojer.**

Dzevad Sabanagic   First Violin
(Head of quartet)
Dzevad is a professor at Sarajevo's music academy. Born in Sarajevo in 1945. He has been leader and first violinist of the quartet since 1967.

Igor Simonji   Second Violin
Born in Osijek in 1958, he completed his course at the music academy under Prof David Kambi. He is also a member of the Sarajevo chamber ensemble and the Sarajevo Philharmonic Orchestra.

Dijana Ihas   Viola
Born in Sarajevo in 1963, she completed her course at the music academy in the class of Prof Dino Sagrestan. She is the first cellist of the Sarajevo Chamber Quartet and philharmonic orchestra.

Nigel Blomiley   Cello
Principlal cellist of the BBC Concert Orchestra, he is a guest at tonight's performance due to the fourth member of the quartet having to remain in Zagreb.

Thank-you for attending tonight's concert. It was arranged at short notice during a visit to Sarajevo in March by EDP Deputy Editor James Ruddy, who was negotiating the rebuilding of the Ljubice Ivezic Orphanage in the city. There he met Professor Nigel Osborne, Head of Music at Edinburgh University, who has close links with the UEA and had been trying to bring the quartet to the UK for over two years. Norwich was chosen as a concert venue in recognition of all the work the region has done for Sarajevo. All proceeds of tonight's concert are in aid of the Sarajevo orphanage rebuilding project by Hope and Homes for Children, a registered charity run by Beccles-born Col Mark Cook, of East Clyffe, Salisbury, Wiltshire, SP3 4LZ.

V

A SOLDIER'S LIFE

Rapid Reaction Force – September 1995

It was to be some months before I would find myself back in Bosnia. I was receiving the occasional note from the friends I had made in Sarajevo. Sometimes returning British soldiers would ring me with messages from the nurses at the Kosevo Hospital or from the orphanage team. I monitored the progress of the project regularly in chats with Mark Cook. He went in a number of times with money stuffed into body belts, sometimes accompanied by Caroline, at great risk. I felt helpless as the television news continued with its accounts of the slaughter across Bosnia.

Then I received a dramatic call on a secure telephone line from southern Croatia. On the other end was a senior British Army officer with the Rapid Reaction Force who was offering me an invitation which no self-respecting journalist would refuse.

'Can you talk privately?' he asked, after introducing himself. 'We're about to break out of here and move up to Mount Igman. How would you like to go with us? You'd be the first journalist to break the news.'

I knew there was a developing respect for the work the *Eastern Daily Press* had been doing in Bosnia. Our ambassador, Robert Barnett, had said as much in Sarajevo. This was confirmation that word had travelled further than I thought.

Since the April concert, I had been continuing with my normal work as the newspaper's deputy editor. That included helping to manage its content and production, as well as bringing along new ideas to maintain its position as England's top-selling morning regional. I was always conscious that I had to strike a balance between our campaigns and aid missions and the core activities of my job. After all, I was paid to direct not to report. But the call from Croatia was intriguing, although I had my grave doubts that it would work out as predicted by the Army officer on the other end.

This was September. The war had been taking some dramatic turns. Peace talks had collapsed. The Bosnian eastern enclaves had fallen to the Serbs with a massacre of thousands in Srebrenica alone. And NATO had finally begun knocking out Serb tanks and ammunition dumps with precision air strikes.

But back in May, what had spurred John Major to positive action had been the humiliation of thirty-three Royal Welch Fusiliers, taken prisoner in their UN blue helmets and paraded for the cameras by the Serbs. He had been incensed enough to appear less than relaxed on the balcony at Lords, whilst watching his favourite game. That evening, during a three hour meeting at Number 10 with Cabinet ministers and senior defence officials, he had made clear that no such degrading scenes should be allowed to happen again in this conflict. He already knew that a rescue by Britain's elite Special Air Service had been ruled out because of the dangers posed to the other 300 UN peacekeepers in Serb hands.

The answer was the deployment of a flexible, high-speed airmobile unit to Croatia to link with the French in a Rapid Reaction Force. This would combine with air power to hit the Serbs quickly, when necessary. That role could cover countering hostage-taking or even providing support to a major pull-out by UN troops. After many delays, the Nato-authorised force, in camouflage green instead of the white and blue of the UN, had placed artillery on Mount Igman to threaten the Serb heavy weapons that had been bombarding Sarajevo for so long. But the main force of 10,000 British and French troops were bottled up at Ploce, a miserable marshy site on Croatia's southern coast. At that point, the Croats were tidying up their own territorial conflicts, having scored some devastating successes against their own rebellious Serb population centres and performed their own ethnic cleansing in the Krajina region. They were deeply suspicious of Nato's aims with the aggressive-sounding new force. They had agreed to lease the site to them, but had prohibited any exercises or training, leaving them effectively stuck there for months. The situation had all the hallmarks of an expensive political foul-up into which the military had fallen.

When I received that private phone call from Ploce, the national tabloids had already been having a field day in criticising the inertia which had befallen the force. The term 'rapid' had even been dropped from the unit's title. The same tabloids would be the first to have savaged John Major if he had directed the force into a mission which had resulted in a steady stream of British soldiers returning home in body bags. The initial momentum behind the deployment had been snuffed out by the threat of such a disaster befalling troops whose role was becoming increasingly unclear.

Despite my doubts, if they were about to break out and join the gunners on Mount Igman, this would be a scoop of some magnitude. On a personal level, I harboured a highly optimistic hope that I would be able to witness the force removing Serbs from the hills around Sarajevo and ending the orphans' suffering. Deep down, I knew it was a fantasy. But I could see myself walking with them along a Sniper Alley where the guns were silent, enjoying ice creams and a tram ride without fearing the worst.

I made some rapid arrangements and was on the next flight into Split, a few miles north of Ploce, where I was picked up by a Land Rover accompanied by the charming Captain Charles Calder, a young career officer in the 1st Battalion Royal Anglian Regiment. Nicknamed The Vikings, the 600-strong unit draws its manpower mainly from my own patch and was providing some of the infantry muscle behind Britain's 4,000-member 24 Airmobile Brigade at Ploce. I had stayed with them previously in Londonderry and had admired their traditions, born of the region's proud county regiments reaching back across the centuries.

Charles, bright, good-looking and with a deceptively easygoing manner, was to be my guide and minder during the coming days.

As we drove that winding road, which skirts the blue waters of the Adriatic for much of Southern Croatia, I was lulled into a false sense of security. Restaurants and bars were open. People were sunbathing in the September sunshine on those once-packed beaches. This was a paradise which the war appeared to have hardly touched. Life was surely idyllic for the men from East Anglia in this veritable paradise. How wrong I was.

Charles put me right very quickly. For five weeks, many of the men had only had an occasional trip off the base to a local cinema or beach. The rest of the time they had been training as well as they could, eating, sleeping and hoping to be ordered to move out from their insect-infested site.

And what a site it was. On my Kummerly and Frey tourist map, it was designated as a watery marsh at the point where the coastal drag meets the road to Mostar. Just a few kilometres north was the existing Bosnian border and the limestone peaks which create violent and sudden weather conditions – a point which was to become very significant in the days ahead.

Already, the huge camp, covered with green tents like some Crimean war tableau, had been swamped by torrential storms from those mountains. Flooding reached up to a metre deep in places, causing evacuation of the troops and a hugely expensive exercise in rebuilding the foundations. Rubble was brought in and the site level raised to avoid similar devastation in the future.

I was given one significant photograph from that past episode. It showed a non-commissioned officer of the Vikings, manoeuvring between the tent lines in the only form of transport suitable, a bright red canoe. It spoke volumes. Here were some of Britain's highly professional soldiers coping with adversity and political inertia as well as they could.

When we reached the camp, it was worse than I thought. As we rounded a corner, two heavy clangs sounded on the Land Rover's metal roof.

'Don't worry,' Charles assured me, 'that's just the local Croat kids using us for target practice with a few well-aimed rocks. We wouldn't feel at home if they packed it in.'

Through the entrance gate, I could see clouds of hot September dust rising from the tent city sloping down to the green marshes, which were intersected by lakes of stagnant brown water that would excite every self-respecting mosquito in the region. To one side were the rusting cranes and shabby warehouses of the former Croatian port area. Swirls of red oxide dust were whipped up by the occasional warm breeze, a remnant of the last bulk carrier to have been unloaded there before the Croats wisely gave up the site.

I was shown to my personal tent which must have been the envy of the battalion. Inside was my allotted camp bed on a pile of wooden pallets to provide extra height protection if the floodwaters returned. Alongside it were several canoes, life preservers and snorkelling equipment. This was the watersports tent. If anything, I was probably the best equipped of anyone on the site to deal with whatever deluge Croatia could throw at us. This confidence, I soon found, was to be proved far from well-founded.

First though was a bolstering mug of tea at the mess tent, the British Tommy's ubiquitous brew-up, which was welcome and friendly. Then there were introductions to the CO, Colonel Roger Brunt, a clear-minded high-flier with ice-blue eyes, who fully expected the unit to be deployed 'up-country,' but tempered that prospect with a note of caution.

'If there is a job to do,' he told me, 'I am sure the battalion will do it very well. Their experience in Northern Ireland will help tremendously.'

'But I would not want it to be a source of pressure to be deployed just because we are here.'

Some of the ordinary soldiers were less measured. One young corporal told me: 'We would like to get up country and put our work into action. That's what we get paid for after all.'

The sense of frustration of some was balanced by the concerns, particularly among the family men, about what might lie ahead. Some were married or had become fathers just before leaving the UK. Others were concerned about the role they would undertake. And it was soon clear that no-one really knew. At the brigade headquarters I was told that the push on Mount Igman was 'imminent'. But it was obvious that this would

The author checking the radio, Sarajevo 1994

Caroline Cook outside the orphanage, Sarajevo 1995

Michael Nicholson and Natasha

The Toy Appeal, Norwich 1996

A Sarajevo orphan, 1995

Geoffrey Cheney, who removed the bullet, Norwich 1996

be as much a political decision as military. And, to complicate matters, it could also involve the French.

As I shared a bottle of decent NAAFI red wine at dinner that evening with Roger Brunt, it was evident that my hoped-for scoop was not to be as clearly defined as I had been led to believe. That night's Sky television pictures brought some cheers of approval from the sizeable audience in the mess tent. They showed Nato air strikes against Serb targets. I began to wonder if this was to be as close as these troops would come to real action in this particular war.

As the days went on and the Igman push came close to materialising only to recede once more beneath the political fog from London, I decided to remain as active as possible. I had brought with me some special editions of the newspaper containing a page of greetings to the Vikings from loved-ones back home. These went down brilliantly with the men, although one claimed he was unable to explain what lay behind the note: 'Your butterfly is missing you'. His mates suspected they knew the answer, but kept it to themselves.

Gradually, in my blue civvies, I was beginning to feel like something of an icon to them, wandering round the camp, taking their pictures, interviewing them, phoning stories home each evening. At least I was an outsider showing an interest. I was also determined to 'muck in' with them, eating at the mess tent, showering in the icy waters of the wooden trestle latrine block, nicknamed 'Ploce Death Camp', and taking part in their activities. I have always been comfortable in the company of soldiers. At one point I agreed to join Roger and Charles in the morning Basic Fitness Test, a three-mile run against the clock around the site.

Finishing within the allotted time, I was confronted by a young private who paid me a supreme compliment: 'Me and the lads think you're mad. Most journos who come here can't wait to get out to a hotel as fast as possible. But you haven't. You're even doing the BFT. You're totally crackers, mate. Totally.'

Despite that, I knew I was a privileged guest. No request was too much for Charles. At one point he came close to fixing for me to travel up to Mostar where I intended to try and trace little Admir Vele, whose shattered leg had been operated on by surgeons in Norwich. British police working with the European monitors in the city had volunteered to help. But the plan fell through because our safety could not be guaranteed.

I did manage to escape from Ploce, however. My saviours were the helicopter pilots of the RAF and 3 Regiment Army Air Corps, who were living at the marsh end of the camp. The latter were based normally at Wattisham, in Suffolk, and welcomed me as a close neighbour.

Initially I was tested out with what was a routine flight in a heavy twin-rotor RAF Chinook which was taking a reconnaissance unit of Royal Anglians to an area near the Bosnian town of Tuzla. The so-called UN safe area had been hit by a Serb rocket the previous May, killing seventy-one civilians, many of them young people gathered in the central cafe area.

Outbound, from Ploce, the mission took us on a terrain-hugging flight, bending and twisting through the mountain valleys between devastated Mostar and Travnik. With the rear ramp open, we could look upward at forests of green pine, as the big bird rattled along at 150 kilometres an hour at what seemed like zero altitude. Our route was never much more than five kilometres from the Confrontation Line between the battling Bosnian and Serb forces. And the RAF crew was taking no chances moving through and over landscape which could harbour a gun position at any turn.

Landing on the runway of the heavily-bombarded town, RAF regulations prevented me from being allowed out of the aircraft. It was on the return leg of the two-hour mission that the aircraft's radar detectors indicated we had been picked up by another monitor and actively 'painted' by an aggressive system.

The exchange of words between the pilot and the door gunner burst through my headphones: 'Fighter, eight o'clock, my side, he has us locked on … Breaking right, into that valley. We'll hide from him behind the hillside …'

I had been invited in to the cockpit earlier and was now watching the horizon swing round drunkenly in the windscreen, as the heavy chopper turned hard to starboard and the ground came up quickly. Swinging wildly, left, then right, the sequence continued for some time until a burst of communication broke the tension. The 'attacking' fighter picked up our constant identification signal, which labelled us as a friendly Nato aircraft. He turned out not to be a renegade Serb jet evading the no-fly ruling but a US carrier based fighter on combat patrol.

It was with some relief that we landed back at Ploce, where it was apparent the civvie in the back had passed the test and had not caused any difficulties.

The prize for this was a scouting mission, this time with the Wattisham boys, again to Tuzla, but with a number of detours in store. After the oppressiveness of the camp, this was to be a real treat. Little did I know what adrenalin-pumping tension really lay ahead.

At the briefing, I was told we would be flying in a Helarm 'two ship' formation, comprising a Rolls Royce-powered Westland Lynx anti-tank helicopter, armed with Tow anti-armour missiles, and a lighter French-built Gazelle scout helicopter, described by the Army Air Corps as 'chic, lissom, athletic …unmistakably foreign'. The two-ship role was adopted to fight Warsaw Pact tanks on the north German plain during the Cold War. The agile Gazelle would bounce around ahead of the Lynx identifying targets at every opportunity. Boffins reckoned that the combined role meant the Lynx was capable of knocking out a tank every thirty seconds in the anticipated conflict which never came. In Bosnia, the same tactics would enable the helicopters to spot and knock out hostile forces or positions anywhere along our route. The mission would take us west of Mostar, up to the high plateau of Tomislovgrad and on to Tuzla where we would land at the local Norwegian UN helicopter base. The return trip would take us to the UN base at Kiseljak for a brief stay, and then back to Ploce. At times we would be very close to the Confrontation Line. This was ill-defined in places and moved from day to day. It was known that the Serbs were smarting after the airstrikes of the past few days and were itching to shoot down aircraft. They had already downed a French Mirage jet and would view a helicopter as more prized quarry for their Surface-to-Air Missile sites. Any doubts I may have had about the potential dangers involved were thrown into sharp relief when I was asked if I could use a ·45 automatic handgun. I had fired one before, but was by no means proficient. The gun was later placed under my seat, presumably for my use in an emergency, but I decided not to inquire. The two crews strapped their weapons in holsters onto their bodies. We all had to recite and memorise a variety of secret radio callsigns. These could save any of us who were still alive after being shot down and needed to call in a rescue chopper. We also rehearsed the procedure we would follow if any of us was taken prisoner. There was always the possibility of captured survivors of a shoot-down being forced to make a false call that would lure an evacuation team into a trap. It was a classic scenario in such a war. We were well prepared for it.

We were also to be accompanied by a tough-looking minder, cuddling his automatic rifle like a long-lost girlfriend. It was clear that we would be opting to defend ourselves forcefully in a crisis. The minder made his views very clear to the civvie who would be complicating his life: 'If we're hit or downed, stick to me like glue. Do what I do. Do what I say.'

Who could argue?

My outward 'taxi' was to be the four-seater Lynx. I was strapped into the rear, with Sgt Ian Griffiths in the pilot's seat. A widely experienced flier, he had that aircrew habit of reducing tension with a well-aimed joke.

After we lifted off, his voice crackled in my headphones: 'If you see flames and a large telegraph pole coming towards us, then please don't hesitate to let me know…'

I had been briefed about the threat from the Serbs' radar-guided SAM bases along the Confrontation Line. The pilot had an unenviable choice. He could hug the contours of the mountainous region and fly the 260 kilometres-an-hour helicopter at thirty metres or less and avoid the missiles. Alternatively, he could climb to 2,000 feet and reduce the chance of being damaged by fire from the ordinary ground troops who would often find a passing chopper a tempting target for their rifles and machine guns. The latter policy was always used to fly across areas known to be occupied by the fundamentalist Muslim Mujahadeen groups who had poured in from Afghanistan to support the Bosnian cause. Their habit when sighting a friendly aircraft was to fire bursts of bullets into the sky in salute. The thick cloud of lead which sometimes resulted had become features marked on the maps of the Army Air Corps fliers. These were definite high-fly zones.

Our outward route took us northward, well away from the Confrontation Line to the east and, theoretically, over the heads of friendly Bosnian forces. On the way back though, we would skirt the ever-changing line and come within easier range of the Serbs.

We began the long climb northward to Tomislovrad, a forbidding and remote UN outpost, 1,300 metres above sea level. Its few troops in thick Arctic parkas and fur gloves were battered almost continuously through autumn and winter by the bitter winds which tore across the Bosnian massif with a wind chill factor that could reach minus 45°C. Their task was to refuel helicopters which had made the ascent from the coast under full load and needed a full tank to extend their range to Tuzla and beyond. After touching down and tanking up, we were immediately racing across the huge Tomislovgrad plateau, an eerie green plain, as flat as a billiard table, where all signs of life appeared extinct. It was there, where Bosnia's southern border comes so close to Croatia, that the fighting had laid waste almost every farm, hamlet and village. A few sheep scattered here and there before the 'thut-thut' thumping of the two helicopters' rotors. But everywhere there were the remains of shattered homes and lives, stretched out like a child's broken and scattered plastic bricks, empty, abandoned. Three years ago, the owners of these once-neat red-roofed villas had expected to live in peace in their idyllic alpine retreats, carving a living from the limestone landscape of sharp crags and soft folds of verdant valleys. Now they were dead or surviving with relatives or fellow refugees, victims of what the men of hate would justify as ethnic cleansing, inventing a new description for an ancient human activity.

Ian and his crew admitted to being moved every time they witnessed such sights. The extent of the devastation had stunned them at first. Even now they found it difficult to understand and accept.

As we barrelled along at 230 kilometres an hour, we were soon through the plain, past Gorni Vakuf, where fighting had turned many homes to rubble, and heading north-east. To our far right, the distant sun was glinting off Mount Igman, where British gunners were occasionally pounding any Serb heavy weapons which fired into Sarajevo. Concentration escalated, as there was now known to be at least one missile battery in range. Through the headphones beneath my heavy helmet, I could hear the comforting tones of a British voice from above: 'Magic, Magic, receiving...'

It was the callsign of the sector's eye-in-the-sky, a long-range AWACS air control plane, flying high above us. Its fourteen-man crew from RAF Waddington in Lincolnshire were ensuring we were friendly and were not being threatened by bandits. Later, we would hear that voice directing the fighters and bombers taking part in one of the rolling NATO airstrikes against Serb communication and supply targets.

Other communications fizzled into my hearing. An American voice. It belonged to an F15 jet pilot who was checking us over. The dialogue was urgent and clear. We knew that one of his air-to-air missiles could be on us in seconds, turning our world into a blinding sheet of flame. No-one was taking any chances.

No unfriendly radar warnings were picked up by the sophisticated protection systems of the Lynx. Near Visoko, we passed over a UN convoy, its white-painted aid lorries kicking up clouds of dust as they swung through the tortuous hairpin bends of a mountain road.

Skirting outcrops of karst limestone at very low level, eyes were peeled for high tension electricity wires. The Lynx co-pilot fed out continuous instructions from his map, like a co-driver in a rally. We all knew a collision with a line at this speed and altitude would be cataclysmic. The chances were increased by the countless twists and turns created by the mountainous features we were crossing. There was also the problem that some lines were not marked on maps. Like spectres, they appeared when we emerged from a ravine and climbed rapidly, just a few metres above them. It was difficult not to be mesmerised, as we wove through exquisitely beautiful high mountain valleys, filled with alpine fir and pine, inhabited by the occasional wild horse or lone cow.

As we hugged the green velvet of one high plateau, the ground suddenly gave way to a sheer 300 metre drop, which brought an 'Ooooh' from our pilot, as my stomach rolled with vertigo. Just his little joke.

Then, as the tall chimney of the coal-burning power plant came into view, he began to sing his version of that well-known Gene Pitney classic, '24 Hours from Tuzla'. Another tension-breaking joke.

The city sprawled before us, its gently rolling contours dotted with villas, a peaceful scene belying its recent history as a centre of refugee overload which was regularly shelled from surrounding Serb bunkers.

Landing at Tuzla's UN headquarters, we were transported to another world, temporarily. This was the helicopter base run by Norbat, the Norwegian unit which had made the sector its home for much of the war. On the flat roofs, stressed-out Scandinavian crewmen, in shorts and aviator goldrimmed shades, could be seen sunbathing on loungers alongside blonde nurses from the medical centre. Inside we were treated to cool Coca Cola in air-conditioned luxury. Our tour also took in the centre's piano room, with a respectable instrument in one corner. The commander also proudly showed us the base's custom-built copy of a Norwegian dockside bar. Its fine wood carvings were bedecked with authentic inner tubes, intended to prevent damage from passing ships. This was hardly likely to be a problem to a bar tucked away in the mountains of Bosnia. But the Norwegians said it all made them feel at home. I wondered what the men of the Royal Anglians at Ploce would have thought of the place. It seemed an idyllic posting and came complete with a teeshirt carrying the message 'Norbat – excellence in action'.

Behind the friendly facade, however, was a unit which was enduring dangers that far outweighed its luxuries. Serb shelling had recently damaged the base. And the previous week one of the unit's sophisticated Bell helicopters had been hit by ground fire, a round passing through the ankle of its navigator.

After an exchange of intelligence – the real reason for our visit – we were lifting off again for the return to Ploce. This time I climbed aboard the glass-fronted Gazelle, a smaller, more manoeuvrable reconnaissance chopper piloted by Lieutenant Julian Facer who was becoming an experienced hand in dealing with the perils of the Bosnian war zone.

We headed south, skirting the Confrontation Line that lay somewhere to our left. In the co-pilot seat Cpl Graeme Nicholson, a Yorkshireman with a wealth of helicopter experience, called out the electricity wires and terrain instructions as we hugged the contours.

The aim this time would be to hug the ground as tightly as possible. The Serb radar operators would be looking for a pair of relatively slow-moving targets just like us. And we would be well within missile range.

Green folds merged into the black and grey of sheer crags through the Plexiglass dome before us in a whirl of colours and textures. We were twisting, left, right, left again, the more powerful matt green Lynx alongside us and then behind us, as we sliced through the valleys and ravines. Suddenly a sheer cliff would emerge ahead. Calmly Graeme would paint a verbal picture of the best way to tackle the climb and necessary descent immediately after we had come through. The engine seemed to be roaring on full power as the small chopper went into a screaming ascent, mercifully sneaking over the lip and down the gentle green slope. The Lynx was immediately behind us.

Then it happened, somewhere south of Kiseljak, our stop-off base, a continuous signal screamed in my headphones. It was a Serb radar operator. He had picked us up, 'painted us' was the jargon, and the signal was our emergency warning. Within seconds, he could be locking on a deadly SAM missile, which could be heading our way.

In the front seats, Julian and Graeme went into a rapid dialogue. Down went the chopper into a steep-sided valley. The screeching stopped. The SAM radar was being blocked by the valley side. Then, after an exchange of words with Ian Griffiths in the Lynx, we hovered, slowly ascending until we were above the cover of the valley side. Back in the open, the screaming began in our headphones again. We popped down once more. More orders were passed and we began a tense game of cat-and-mouse which seemed to last for hours. Up, screech. Down, silence. Up, silence, then screech when the radar man picked us up again. Down, silence. Throughout it all, the two helicopters were progressing southwards, the occasional burst of communication coming from the 'Magic' AWACS crew, high in the sky, who had also picked out the missileman's radar activity with their sensitive electronics. Now came the deadly poker game which was being played. To gain a viable 'fix' on us, the Serb radar man had to transmit aggressively, providing the AWACS with a target. He knew that. We knew that. If the target was precisely identified as hostile, the RAF crew could summon in a US F15 armed with anti-radar missiles which would target the radar's own beam and wipe out the base. I had been told of just such an episode during out visit to the Norbat base. An officer explained how a nearby radar base had been fought over, captured and recaptured many times by the Bosnians and Serbs. 'Then, one day,' he said, 'in came the F15s and boom, the top of the mountain was ten metres lower.'

I understood a little of what was happening. Julian and Graeme were keeping me informed by describing their manoeuvres. Two sharp and focused professionals, they went through the various sequences with precision. It was comforting to see them in action. I felt cocooned by the machine. It was the same air of unreality which had come to me before in Sarajevo, when the anti-aircraft gun was being fired across the junction. Men who fought on the Western Front in the Great War have sometimes spoken about their feelings of detachedness from the scene of carnage when they were running through no man's land. This was nothing like the horrors they experienced. But, like their's, my mind seemed to be attempting to blot out the dangers.

Then it stopped. We popped up from a clearing and the headphone screech had gone. 'Maybe he got bored,' was Julian's wry observation as he gunned the Gazelle onward to Kiseljak.

Just as we began to settle down from the experience, the UN-marked base came into view beneath us in a natural bowl in the rolling limestone hills. This was to be just a quick touch-down and take-off after a brief exchange with the UN team there.

As Julian hovered the machine into its drop onto the big white H on the pad below, Julian and I were keeping our eyes open for obstructions. Then I noticed a man standing midway up a rocky path to our left, aiming a shoulder-held cylinder straight at us.

'What's that?' I blurted. 'Looks like someone with a missile. Left, left.'

Graeme turned in his seat to look back toward me, broke into a big smile and then spoke through his mouthmike: 'Don't worry James. I'd spotted him. He's got a TV camera and he's filming us. We're going to be famous, not dead.'

It was one of the few light moments on the trip. It was with some relief that we touched down soon after at Ploce. I knew Julian and Graeme would require several pints of beer from me to ensure the story of my mistake with the TV cameraman did not become 'the legend of the journo in the back seat'. That's the way with the quiet heroes who were doing so much to bring peace to Bosnia.

That evening, I returned to the Royal Anglians and found that I was being upgraded from the one star watersports tent to sharing one of the four star two-man tents in the officers' row, close to the CO. Could this mean promotion for the journo? No, it emerged later, the men needed more space for their sports gear. Still, I was now feeling pretty integrated, having even been bequeathed some flip flops by the quartermaster for my towel-draped hikes to and from the freezing shower.

During my relocation, I noticed that my new camp bed was not on pallets and decided to take an added precaution in case of flooding. I fixed all my valuable gear to the tent roof poles. That included passport, money, flight tickets, camera equipment and a new Dell laptop computer which I was road-testing.

After a very acceptable dinner, Charles took me to the Sergeants' Mess for a drink and some lively banter. On the way back up the site, I noticed a towering pillar of thick grey cloud gathering very rapidly just out to sea, accompanied by frequent bolts of lightning. With a storm brewing, I congratulated myself on my precautions with my valuables, brushed my teeth, took off my clothes and climbed into my sleeping bag.

It was probably an hour later after I had fallen into a deep sleep, partly induced by a couple of beers and half a bottle of that NAAFI red wine again, that it happened. They call it the Bora and it hits you like a fast train, a wind that bursts in uninvited, with just the black sky and lightning as a warning, delivering a thunderous jet of numbing cold. It was the hailstones which came first and woke me, heavy grape-sized baubles, thumping hard on the thick canvas roof. My eyes blinked open. Sheets of white, lingering lightning lit up the gap in the tent flap. Then the whole structure began to rock as the first winds struck at what was later esti-mated to be ninety kilometres an hour. Still lying helplessly, I began to hear shouting, crashing sounds, then a ping, another ping and several more as my heavy tent pegs gave way. With disbelief, I then saw the whole tent rise up, carrying my valuables with it, and fly over my head toward the perimeter fence, thirty metres away. In the white flashes I looked to my right and immediately saw most of the row of officers lying in their cots, without tents, stunned by the rapidity of the natural forces which had struck. Then came the ferocity of the hailstones and raindrops, thousands of small and larger pins, biting at my exposed face and torso in a whirl of sound and wind.

The icy cold brought me to my senses. I noticed an object flying over me, as the flashes came almost simultaneously. The perimeter fence resem-bled an overstretched washing line as what remained of the heavy canvas tents were being ripped and further battered on the heavy strands of wire.

It was time to leave. I jumped out of the sleeping bag and staggered toward the communal tent of the junior officers nearby. It was named in honour of a raunchy nightclub back at home base in Colchester and offered the same kind of music in the evenings. After heaving open the rear flap I peered inside and saw four of them, young lieutenants, clinging like fruit bats to the roof supports. With every new burst of wind, they were rising at least a metre off their beds as the huge tent strained and slid upwards on its loosened guy ropes.

'James, grab a bloody support quickly, we need all the weight we can get,' screamed one, whose eyes were bulging with the effort of clinging on.

'Not bloody likely,' I shouted back. 'Get out while you can. The bloody thing's going to take off and you'll all go with it.'

With that I did a quick reverse through the flap and clawed my way round the front. As I went I noticed something long and metallic fly past my head, clanging against a thick square lump. It was one of the steel tent braces attached to its concrete base and must have weighed twenty kilos.

It was likely that no tent would withstand the Bora. So I decided to avoid them. I staggered across to my rocking camp bed, picked up my rucksack and remaining gear and made off, aimlessly, into the storm. Then I remembered the bomb shelter I had been shown on arrival. This was a metal freight container, surrounded by sandbags. Due to the alert condi-tion of the base such shelters had to be ready in case of an attack from Serb ground-to-ground missiles or heavy artillery. They were within range of

Ploce at that time, in theory anyway, although no-one worried too much about them. Through the sheeting, whipping rain and wind, I dragged my freezing body to the container and fell inside its open double door. The resourceful Charles was already there, rigging up a light and sleeping areas. 'Oh, James, how nice to see you. Bloody rough one eh?' he quipped, then went back to the light.

Also there was another officer, who had been meticulous enough to bring many of his belongings with him. Among them, I noticed amid the lightning flashes, was a family-sized plastic carton of biodegradable washing powder, an item I felt showed a highly commendable degree of forward planning.

After some discussion, the three of us had rearranged the container to provide relatively comfortable sleeping areas. We agreed, with some wisdom, that there was little we could do until morning. So we took the sensible course, and settled down for some slumber. The only difficulty was keeping dry. The rain was still battering the sturdily-built metal box. But it had come to the camp second-hand from the Croats and had several shrapnel holes which were letting in water. We each changed position until we felt we were safe from the dripping and settled down for sleep.

Then came the explosion. It was muffled, like a distant grenade going off inside a concrete bunker. Each of us sat up immediately. 'Christ, what was that!' shouted Charles.

I could feel my face and hands were coated with a strange substance, so too were the faces of the two others, white, almost like a chemical covering. There also appeared to be a cloud inside the container. I suspected poison gas, which would have been deadly in our unprotected condition. We dashed for the door, swung it open and aimed our torches inside.

There on the floor under a shrapnel hole was the source of the trouble. The exotic wash powder had taken in a steady stream of water from the puncture in the roof. There had been a reaction causing pressure to build up. Eventually the lid had blown off and the whole interior had been covered in a fine cloud of white granules.

We laughed with uncontrolled relief when the cause emerged, cleaning the coating off our bodies and faces with whatever cloths we could find.

'I don't bloody well believe this,' groaned Charles at last. 'First the bloody storm and now we're attacked by bloody wash powder. Talk about a night to remember.'

Next morning, the top end of the camp looked like it had been blitzed. Tents had disappeared completely. They had hung on the fence wire for a time and then flown off into the distance. Wooden pallets were lying splintered everywhere. Beds, clothes, books, bottles, food and valuables were strewn across the ground. Steel and aluminium poles, six centimetres in diameter, were lying crushed and twisted like drinking straws. And everywhere soldiers had begun clearing up, washing and discussing their night of hell.

In bright sunshine on a calm September morning I searched for my own valuables and, miraculously, found them under what was left of my soggy canvas tent just inside the fence. I laid out the Deutschmarks, passport, air tickets and camera body and lenses to dry on the container's sandbag wall. The Dell laptop was there too, still in its black canvas case after a journey of some thirty metres at high speed. After a night in the pounding rain, it looked remarkably well. I could not resist opening it up, hitting the power button and waiting. Remarkably, the unit hummed to life and the screen lit up, bringing up all its original functions, still visible through a film of moisture.

I left its sensitive electronics to dry out, completely baffled at its survival.

Further down the slope, the private soldiers had escaped the worst of the storm for some reason. Most tents were intact, a fact which gave rise to some ribaldry when they learned that the officers had taken such a pasting. This fact was driven home with some glee by some of the men, who had absorbed the worst of the flooding two weeks earlier when the officers had escaped. Nature, they chuckled, was the great equaliser.

Elsewhere on Camp Ploce, the devastation was equally varied. Official figures at 24 Airmobile Brigade Headquarters told the story: cookhouses destroyed, twenty Royal Engineers slightly injured, tents completely missing. Scores of soldiers received treatment from being crushed or struck by the flying poles and rocks. Some received stitches for head wounds, but the worst was a broken arm. There were many stories of near misses, one involving a young private who had left his bed seconds before a fence post had pierced the tent roof and embedded itself in his mattress. So impressed were his colleagues that I was invited to observe the scene and take a photograph with my still soggy camera. Other casualties included the brigade church, which was registered as having taken off and disappeared. The worst effects appeared to have been among the French helicopters, one of which had been tipped on its side and others damaged.

But such adversity always brings out the best in the British Tommy. The blow, in some ways, helped to lift the air of stagnation at the camp, forcing men to act decisively and employ their training in a rebuilding exercise. It was significant that one of the first buildings to be re-erected at the Royal Anglians' encampment was the Sergeants' Mess, complete with bar and card tables. It was with some amusement that I was standing later with Charles in the frenzy of Brigade headquarters and heard an officer remark: 'Better not let the Press get hold of this one.'

In his inimitable way, Charles smiled, turned to him and remarked: 'Too late old chum, the Press is already here and lost his tent last night.'

The following day, I dried out my sodden gear, packed up and handed over to Charles a parting bottle of decent Irish whiskey that I had been nursing all week and which had survived the Bora. It was with some sadness that I offered my thanks and goodbyes to Roger Brunt, the CO, and the many officers and men who had made me a part of their world.

Igman had never been a firm option, it later emerged. But I had been given a unique insight into the life of a force which was poised for action which would never come. Their raw-edged humanity in the face of war and natural disaster had simply reinforced my respect for them. They had continued to train hard in many ways for a conflict which held many unseen perils. I had always had an unshakable respect for the professionalism and attitude of Britain's fighting men. I had developed this view close-up many times, witnessing them at work and play from locations as diverse as Northern Ireland, Gibraltar and the Falklands. I had also seen it already from the troops wearing the blue helmets of the UN. When they gave children sweets and rebuilt orphanages, it was not because they were ordered to do so. They wanted to help, deep down, sincerely. They hated the cruelty that was being meted out to innocents. Whether through peacekeeping in the white vehicles of UN mandate or through fighting the aggressors in the matt green and black of the Royal Anglians, many had a strong desire to use their training to help. Before I left Ploce, one young rifleman from Norfolk summed it up perfectly. In the time-honoured cliché style which he felt a journalist might understand, he exclaimed: 'We just want to get stuck in. You know, do our bit instead of kicking our heels. People expect it. We expect to have to do it. So let's get on with it.'

As I was whisked off in a Lynx to meet my flight at Split, I reflected on the political stagnation which had left so many eager men bottled up in a hellish swampy site for so long. As John Major and Foreign Secretary Douglas Hurd knew only too well, the Vietnam war had taught everyone the perils of what the Americans aptly termed 'mission creep', wherein a fixed political and military strategy had escalated alarmingly to accommodate an increasingly elusive objective. The resulting body bags had led to the defeat of the world's mightiest superpower.

Our political leaders did not want to repeat the exercise in Bosnia.

At the same time, people were demanding action. Emotionally and reasonably, ordinary British citizens were sickened by the carnage on Europe's doorstep. I was convinced that the answer was to force the warring sides to the peace conference table with air power, knocking out their key weapons with little risk of body-bag backlash.

Yes, the children of Sarajevo needed help to end their suffering. But there was a clear and incisive way to provide it. Even from my narrow perspective on the ground, I was becoming increasingly convinced that it should not be at the cost of the lives of the courageous and eager young men at Ploce.

VI

HE MUST HAVE BEEN A BRAVE MAN

Sarajevo – December 1995

It must have been one of the most dangerous jobs in the world. In the dark of night, a painter would climb a tall ladder and add protective coats of colour to the woodwork on the very pinnacle of Sarajevo's main orphanage. On top of a 600 metre hill above the city, it was possible from his precarious perch to see the tracer bullets and mortar blasts that would flash across the front lines, just a short distance away.

He must have been a brave man. He was also lucky. Somehow he survived his shifts with his paintbrush during those long and freezing nights. Others were not so lucky, as our project to rebuild the home proceeded rapidly throughout the year. On a bright May day, one of the trustees at the orphanage, Branko Radojevic, had been helping a builder to erect a new gate when a mortar bomb had landed in the adjoining netball court. Both he and the workman were caught in the open. Shrapnel tore into them, leaving the builder with critical internal wounds and Branko badly cut but not seriously injured. In his calm and optimistic voice, Hilma, the banker for the rebuilding project, told me in a rare telephone call that it had been a miracle that none of the home's forty-four orphans had been playing outside or in the netball court at the time.

'Many of them have been so frightened recently that they have gone back to the basement for cover,' he said.

'The fire crews have pumped out the basement. It was full of stinking water and filth. The children have helped clear out the mess to try and make it habitable for the young ones, nine of whom are babies.

'There is little water, electricity and gas, so they are living in a kind of hell. There is little wood for fuel, but they have set up a chimney to try and cook some hot meals. It is awful. But the children are hoping that there are still people who care and are trying to help them.

106

'I have not been able to get up and see them every day because of the heavy firing. Wednesday has been the worst day for us so far. Bombs and shells have been falling almost every minute, some of them heavy calibre, unusually heavy. We have a strict curfew and the whole city has been hiding in their cellars to try and stay alive.'

It was typical of Branko that he would have been trying to help the builder. An orphan, he had spent much of his life in the home. At twenty-two, he feared privately that his time had come to face the loneliness and uncertainty of life on the outside. With no other friends, the home had become a rock of hope for the quiet, white-coated Bosnian, who hoped he might make the progression from resident orphan to resident staff member without anyone questioning his right to do so. 'All I want is to help, wherever I can, just help,' he had told me.

The rebuilding project had threatened that hope. On my first visit, he had revealed his fears, quietly, his eyes filled with pleading. During a lull in the shooting, we had walked outside, to the playground where he had shown me the shrapnel holes in the rusting see-saw. He had also shown me the mortar holes from previous near-misses. He had been too frightened to discuss the unmistakable mortar pits which I had also noticed in the playground. These had been dug and partly sandbagged by the Bosnians and had drawn the fire of the opposing Serbs. They were empty on that visit. But I suspected they would be used from time to time, not only for their marvellous tactical position overlooking the enemy positions, but also as a propaganda device. By bringing in retaliatory fire from the Serbs, they would create emotional headlines. Such was my developing cynicism about the war. I suspected there were those in the Bosnian government who felt a direct hit on the home and the rebuilding project would be far more useful than the completion of the scheme. The Serbs may have exerted many cruelties against the city. But they were not fools. Why would they turn their attentions on the orphanage if they had not been provoked? It was a question which would remain unanswered. And a builder along with the unfortunate Branko had become victims in the game.

That summer had seen a number of cataclysmic events. The fall of Srebrenica, in July, had been the blackest day in the history of the UN's involvement in Bosnia. The Serbs had ejected 13,000 women and children, who had gathered finally in makeshift camps at Tuzla airport, after the slaughter of many thousands of their menfolk. Aerial photographs later released by the US showed four mass graves near Srebrenica, containing as many as 4,000 men and boys. Many had been shot. The Croats, too, recaptured the entire 'Krajina' region, ejecting at least 150,000 local Serbs.

In August, a mortar bomb, allegedly fired by the Serbs, struck another crowded Sarajevo marketplace, killing thirty-seven and wounding eighty-eight. It also provoked a reaction which had been long hoped-for by many parties to this bitter struggle. Heavy rolling airstrikes were launched by Nato, forcing the deflated Serbs to withdraw much of their heavy weaponry from around the city. A US-led 'battle of the maps' also began, with the warring sides attempting to negotiate their best allocation in a carve-up of the country before the inevitable peace could be declared.

Before the heavy guns and mortars were pulled back, many more statistics were created. Seven people were slaughtered in Dorbrinja, Sarajevo's pitiful Olympic village suburb which we had passed through in our travels to and from the airport. They had been standing in a queue for water in a school hall when a mortar bomb had been lobbed through a hole in the roof caused by a previous shelling. At least ten people were left badly maimed.

In a phone call from the city, I was told of another statistic. The daughter of the orphanage cook had been killed when a mortar bomb had struck their home. She was just twelve. She had managed to survive the long years of siege until fate had snuffed out her life with the 'winning tape' almost in sight. I hardly knew her but I felt a terrible hatred in my heart for her murderers. That hate was being directed into doing what little I could for the living.

Mark and Caroline Cook had been in regular contact through this awful period. Cheques were pouring in for the project from across East Anglia and the rest of the UK. Both of them had been continuing their risky trips into the city with cash instalments to keep the project moving. I was doing fund-raising talks wherever possible and writing news stories to publicise the children's plight. Prayers were being said for the orphans at churches across the country. As the work went on, new children began to be admitted to the home. Some were coming from the Bosnian eastern enclaves of Srebrenica, Zepa and Gorazde which the UN had declared 'safe havens' and the Serbs had overrun. One was an orphan, just three days old, whose father had been killed in Gorazde and whose mother had also died. There were now nearly fifty of them living in the hellish conditions of the basement.

By the autumn, the British and US governments managed to force the warring sides to the conference table for the long-awaited deal that would bring a kind of lasting peace. The Dayton agreement of November proposed a division of the country with 51 per cent to go to the federation forged by the Bosnians and their relatively recent allies, the Croats. The remaining 49 per cent went to Karadzic's Bosnian Serbs. Making it stick would become a minefield and the introduction of IFOR, the Implementation Force, by the UN, would be crucial.

This coincided with the completion of the orphanage project. For once, I hoped to go to Sarajevo for a celebration instead of a wake. I felt such joy and a little pride at knowing that so many people had helped to create a civilised home for children who had suffered so much hardship.

This time we would not have to fly in via Maybe Airlines. Baroness Chalker had agreed to perform the opening ceremony and had laid on vehicles from her Overseas Development Administration, to take us from Split airport through Mostar and over the mountains into Sarajevo.

There were four of us in the group, myself, Mark, Caroline and their son William, who was at university and aiming to become a Parachute Regiment officer.

Our driver, Drago, was one of those dour, dark-haired and very dependable Sarajevans who would talk about near-death experiences as if he was discussing the football results. His favourite story was his recent escape on Sniper Alley when he had been shot in the neck while driving a soft-skinned vehicle. His high-collared bulletproof jacket had taken the impact and the rifle round had embedded itself in the kevlar armoured collar. Ever since then, Drago liked to wear polo necks.

He greeted us as we landed at Split, his sad expression empathising with the vehicle he was driving: a white ODA armoured Land Rover with the offside window completely shattered but, thankfully, not penetrated, by a past engagement with an unfriendly gunman.

As we drove north up the Neretva valley to Mostar, I was given a close view of the devastation I had seen from the air in the helicopter trips from Ploce. In some villages, Croatian homes were smashed and blackened by fire, whilst the Bosnian villas remained intact, their present occupants harvesting late season vegetables from the once-neat flower gardens. In other places, the reverse had happened, with Croats having displaced Bosnians.

The realities of this war had never truly reached the British public. It was far too complex for us to understand fully. History had lit the fuse, but the explosives had been prepared by many hands. How had so many men decided to turn against old friends and neighbours purely on the grounds of their ethnic grouping? It was more than mere racial hatred. At a purely local level, old scores had indeed been settled between clans. But there had also been the greed of power-hungry warlords, who had shown no allegiance to anyone except their own bank accounts. In the vicious fighting of the Bihac pocket, Croat commanders had even instituted a rent-a-gun system. This involved their heavy weapons being turned on the Bosnians or the Serbs, depending on who was the highest bidder on any particular day.

Nothing surprised me any more. It was the reason I decided never to discuss the strategy of the war in any detail. I concentrated instead on what I could understand, the suffering of the orphans.

Like some returning parent, I was looking forward to seeing them again. I had loaded several ex-Army kitbags with goodies for the opening party we had planned. As we rolled across those snow-covered valleys filled with natural beauty and ugliness, I was anticipating the pleasure we would bring to those young faces. And for once they would be at peace.

It was when our Land Rover approached a checkpoint to our right, that I was reminded of the fragility of this particular peace. The striped pole, guarded by a group of young Bosnian soldiers, marked the start of the Mount Igman road into Sarajevo. Since it had been fought over and taken by the Bosnians, the steep and winding track had become the only major land artery, bringing in everything from aid to weapons. It had been a frightening journey in which many had died on the reverse slope. Exposed to Serb gunfire, travellers had taken to driving or running as fast as possible down the long and exposed stretches.

On this day, I noticed an old man passing through the descending barrier, he was loaded like a mule, two giant panniers hanging from his sloping shoulders. He was about to make the thirty-mile walk through the snow instead of opting for the 'safe passage' that was now supposed to have been guaranteed through Serb territory. Such was the mistrust of peace deals.

Our own passage through the front lines was smoother. The Bosnians waved us on. In an ODA white vehicle, we were protected and privileged beyond the hopes of the old man. I felt some guilt at that thought. But I knew that there could still be trouble from the purple and black uniformed Serb guards who checked our papers at their own barrier. They joked with Drago, a Bosnian, as we paused in a zone of total destruction. I was reminded of the pictures of Flanders in the Great War, where a few scorched trees were the only visible upright structures. Like the trenchline Tommies, these men had adapted to their surroundings. Amid the carnage, they were still able to joke. Perhaps that made an encouraging point about the resilience of the human psyche. Perhaps the point was far more sinister. They had become impervious to horror.

Passing through what was now the Serb suburb of Illidza I wondered if I would be able to spot the home which had been owned by Vesna Halebic, the orphanage scheme's architect, and her carpenter husband Osman. She had given us the address, shown us pictures and explained its location. She knew a Serb family would now be savouring its comforts and wonderful carved wood features. She also wondered if they would have discovered her family's life savings, buried beneath the rose bush in the garden.

But we did not see it. And we were not intending to stop. Illidza was one district of the city which the Dayton deal would hand back to the Bosnians. We knew the Serbs there would be angry and unpredictable.

Rounding a foggy turn, we were given a welcome: three loud crashes resounded off the sides and roof of the heavy vehicle. It was not snipers, just Serb children throwing snowballs from a bridge. Was this the time-honoured mischief of the young? I could not help thinking of the parallels with the stone-throwing Croat children in Ploce. This was a land where the children hurled inert objects at peacekeepers, whilst their fathers had matured into firing rifles and rockets. It was called growing up.

Sarajevo was its depressing self in the late afternoon blanket of fog, which was often kept in place by the surrounding hills. It was an irony throughout the siege that people prayed for ugly foggy days such as this. It clouded the vision of the snipers and mortarmen.

Drago pulled up outside our old apartment block, where we made arrangements for the next few days. Before he left, he made his first and last personal statement: 'I am pleased the orphanage project has been carried out. But what will happen in the future nobody knows. Nobody.'

And he was right. Over the coming days we were greeted with a mixture of guarded optimism tempered with real fears that the deal would not stick.

Vesna joined us and helped us find more presents for the party. We paid in Deutschmarks for the few balloons and streamers that were to be found in the sparsely filled shops.

When we visited the children, I was sorry to see they were still unable to use the new bedrooms and rest areas created by the rebuilding scheme. They were living in the decrepit Dickensian ageing part of the building because of the lack of heating oil for the rebuilt area. The director was reluctant to move them in until the oil arrived and the system was properly tested. It seemed a harsh policy with Christmas approaching. But there were some policies which we foreigners were unable to countermand.

The whole building was still a grim relic of Communist utilitarianism. But inside, the rebuilt section had been turned into a comfortable, modernised base for those tiny babies and teenage waifs who had lost so much, including the love of a real home and parents to cherish them. That was still missing. We recognised the need to instil greater affection into the institutionalised regime that existed there. But that would be for the future. For the present, a hovel had been turned into an anchor for children drifting in a sea of hate. That was an important beginning. And some of the children knew what we had done.

As they clamoured for attention, I passed out the Take That music tapes which I had promised I would bring them, together with some cassette players and the all-important batteries in a city still without such luxuries. To some extent the teenagers were the most vulnerable, not the babies.

The latter were receiving the basic requirements, together with a measure of love from the staff. The older children were the lost ones. And they would remain so. It was a cruel irony for many of them that the war which had caused their individual tragedies, removing their parents and their homes, had also provided the safety net of humanitarian aid in which they could suspend themselves. Peace would bring questions about their futures without such attendant sympathy and assistance. For many that was scary.

It was a fear encapsulated with great articulation by one of the leaders of their group, Suleyman, eighteen. He was a soft-spoken boy with close-cropped hair and blue eyes who had been abandoned at birth and had known institutions for most of his life.

'The war has been frightening, but it has also brought us together in many ways. I do not know what will happen in the future. Some of us are quite old now and will have to leave. But where do we go?

'Everyone has many problems, too many to care about us. We have no-one else. But we have known only this and have no idea of what life is like outside.

'We have seen such kindness from the people in England who have given us our new home. But soon I will have to go. It will be taken from me before I have enjoyed it. That is hard to take.

'I do not want to say anything else, only that I am grateful for everything people have done. All I have in the world to give is my thanks. That is what I will give. I cannot say anything more ...'

He was close to tears. But he would not cry. He could not let the others see that. In some ways it would remove his quiet authority over this group. He was sensitive enough to know that it would also demoralise them to see a leader depressed and uncertain about where they were all going.

For Mark and Caroline, this would become a major issue for the future. They would battle to ensure the older children were given the support, work and accommodation needed to take their first adult steps in life. It was to prove to be a hellishly difficult struggle in a land where Titoesque attitudes had provided only the basic support for the illegitimate, the abandoned and the true orphans which its otherwise orderly society had thrown up. They had been outcasts, as if their position was of their own making. Now some feared a return to those values.

For the moment though I was pleased that the structural work had been carried out so professionally by Vesna and Osman's building team, despite the war. Lighting, heating, water supplies had all been fed into the rebuilt rooms, which included cosy bunk rooms and single bedrooms for the older children. Posters of Madonna and other pop stars already adorned some of the walls. And there were already a few home-made soft toys for the toddler play area.

It was a heartening experience for the four of us to see the work almost complete. The one great problem was the cold. The Serbs were refusing to allow a tanker of oil through their lines, which meant the children faced a Christmas in temperatures well below freezing point. After the horrors of the basement, it seemed a small problem for them. And whatever negotiations we held with the authorities over the coming days were to prove fruitless.

There would be another disappointment on the visit. It concerned Mark and Caroline's son, William. A well-travelled and adventurous young man, he had expected his first visit to Sarajevo to be accompanied by at least a little gunfire.

It was an understandable wish for someone who would be joining one of Britain's elite fighting forces in the near future. From one perspective, the threat of violent death provides a test of your personal strength that nothing else can match. I had felt it several times and did not wish to repeat the experience. But for someone joining the Army shortly, it would be a near-vital requirement. Despite the quiet, it was with some trepidation that I agreed to join William on a ride on one of the city's trams. They were running once more, passing the mangled wreckage of those which had not survived the siege. The only previous occasion I had stepped aboard one of the red cars had been in a rare and foolish gesture of solidarity with these people. At the time the trams were being shot up regularly by Serb gunners. But I wanted to join Sarajevans who were making a statement about freedom and defiance. All the time I had been waiting for the bullets to tear through the dusty windows in what was one of the longest short journeys of my life.

This time, there were no bullets. Just William enjoying the experience, fascinated by the scale of the bombardment which had left huge concrete and glass buildings in pieces, scorched and shattered, for mile after mile. It had felt safe. The vehicle was packed with humanity, from soldiers to old women with a few groceries in shopping bags. For the first time, I was able to relax and marvel at the way cafe society was returning to the pavement and alleyway tables.

But I was misled. The following day, a Serb gunner fired into a tram, once again near the Holiday Inn. And once again a woman was hit in the eyes. As the generals were handing over control of the city from the white-painted UN to Nato's camouflage green Implementation Force at the airport, the Serbs decided to make a statement symbolising their continuing potency as a force for evil. The result was a young mother being carried to the Kosevo Hospital, bleeding and blinded. And, once again, the trams stopped for a time.

That night at the apartment we ate some of the awful dried dishes I had brought from England, a minestrone with extra noodles concoction which would have made any army surrender. The electricity was coming on occasionally. Water was more of a problem. We were still filling barrels and bottles for the couple of hours each day that it ran. Caroline decided we should have a pot of tea and poured a bottle into a pan to boil.

'There's nothing like a good steaming drink to lift the spirits,' said the woman who knew all about the Army's affection for such a brew.

Pouring the whole bottle into the pan, she switched up the gas and began sorting out the mugs and pot.

After a couple of minutes, I began to sniff something odd: 'Is that gas leaking? I'm sure there's an odd smell, slightly sweet. Do they put an odour in their gas here like they do in England?'

Caroline began to sniff out the offending source in the tiny kitchen.

'It doesn't seem to be the gas,' she observed. 'Maybe something is burning and stuck to the cooker.'

We both began sniffing now. William also joined in. Then Mark came through, his nostrils twitching like radar aerials.

'Darling, are you burning something?'

'No, James thinks it might be gas. But I can't smell a leak from the pipes or cooker.'

Then William and I sniffed our way along the cooker to the pan of boiling water.

'Cor,' said the future para officer, 'that's not water in the pan. It's spirit.'

'What?' exclaimed Mark, sniffing the steam from the offending liquid. 'Phew. You're right. He's right. It's neat Slivovic from that empty bottle.'

He whisked the pan off the heat, not taking any chances, as we roared with laughter at what would have been one of the strongest pots of tea we would have ever experienced.

Next day came the official opening of the home. We turned up early and decked out the inside with the contents of my kitbags, together with the streamers we had bought. The children all joined in. Suleyman directing operations, laying the tables carefully with plastic cutlery, red napkins, hats and novelties. It was a frenzy of excitement, the first most had known in four years. It was also a media event. Bosnian television came along, as did the BBC and Colin Baker, of Britain's flagship News at Ten programme.

The cameras zoomed in on the small faces covered with stains from the Yorkie bars, Smarties and crisps which I had been given by Tesco for the event. Many of the children appeared totally dumbfounded by the experience. The younger ones ate the sweets and cakes with complete abandon. Some of the older children were more reserved, saving the chocolate for the privacy of their rooms. Others, including Suleyman, did not want to take part. I found him on the stairwell, outside the main meeting room, brooding and contemplative.

I begged him to join the party, but he was adamant. 'James, I do not want to offend you. But I cannot celebrate a future I do not know exists. I cannot perform in that way for television cameras. Outside I would be happy. Inside I would be sad. I am sorry.'

It was a genuinely intuitive observation for a youngster whose maturity belied his years. I decided not to cajole him and his three teenage friends any further. Instead, I brought them each drinks and a goodie bag of chocolate. They accepted with an outward show of reluctance that their more senior position demanded.

There was a moment of raw emotion when the leader of the Sarajevo String Quartet turned up.

He hugged me warmly and recalled fondly the concert at Norwich Cathedral as well as our meal afterward in the Indian restaurant when the bizarre strippagram girl had turned up. No-one spoke as the haunting notes of the Adaggio filled his violin. Even the children paused at their placemats to take in the sound that had become entwined with the image of their city's suffering.

As I watched their faces, some open-mouthed with fascination, it was hard to imagine how it had been three years earlier. Of that time, the *Sunday Times* journalist Janine Di Giovanni had written: 'The orphanage was probably the worst place, aside from the morgue, in Sarajevo.

'It was Dickensian, dank, smelled of sour boiled food although there was hardly any food at all in the filthy kitchen … There were rats, cold, wet, oily floors and rain poured in the open windows blown out by the impact of shells.

'There were no toilets; the children rarely washed and their hair was matted with dirt. They slept eight or nine to a room; some had beds, others had sleeping bags piled in a corner.'

When Lady Chalker arrived to perform the opening ceremony, her small figure was sensibly insulated by a thick blue coat, with a Russian-style fur hat, boots and gloves. Later that day she would pledge a further £20 million in humanitarian aid to Bosnia. The home project must have appeared like a pinprick alongside such spending. But she was fully aware of its symbolic importance.

Her ministry had done a great deal to help oppressed people who had little influence in a world where aid is so often given in return for political favours. With courage she had assisted the persecuted and powerless Kurds of Iraq. Despite the reluctance of Douglas Hurd's Foreign Office, she had also empowered her own people in Bosnia to help the victims where possible.

Here, high on a hill overlooking the burned shell of the once free and beautiful city of Sarajevo, was a small but significant symbol of that help in action.

As she toured the old section of the orphanage, she absorbed the scene before her with some dignity. With fresh snow poking through shellholes in the roof, she saw how up to six children were sleeping in dingy bedrooms, where the cold was kept out by just a few grubby brown blankets. Rubble and twisted metal lay on the damp floors amid the few books and clothes of their occupants.

Downstairs she brought a smile to the face of a tousle-haired toddler who had been crying. Hugging him tightly, he soon forgot his tears and began to play with one of her earrings. His tears were forgotten as he giggled along with her at their new game.

This was not a politician taking part in a photo opportunity. She looked like she might never let go. Her entourage of armed security men and senior civil servants began to wonder if she ever would, as they coughed their urgent coughs, indicating their anxiety about their timetable.

But encased in that Muscovite fur hat, her beaming face told its own story. This was a woman who truly cared.

As she toured the newly rebuilt section of the home, she paid a sincere tribute to the work done on the £200,000 contract. And she paid a personal tribute to my own newspaper's readers.

'I think it's marvellous. We have to be careful to co-ordinate and to make maximum use of the aid which is given by individuals.

'That is why it is absolutely first-class for the *Eastern Daily Press* to pioneer this help for Mark and Caroline Cook's orphanages.

'Your newspaper has developed an international reputation for delivering aid in this way, not just as a short-term fix, but in a sustained way.'

It was then she paused and had a ministerial brainwave.

'James,' she confided, 'What these children want now is toys to play with. Why don't you run an appeal for some?'

I hesitated. This was not an occasion for a 'Yes, Minister' response. The Christmas Convoy appeal had unleashed a huge tide of giving among the newspaper's readers. It had nearly proved overwhelming.

'It's a wonderful idea, Lady Chalker,' I muttered. 'But we will probably get tonnes and tonnes of toys.'

She flicked a hand in an upward motion, dismissing my pathetic concerns.

'Don't worry, we can can give them to the children of Sarajevo. You supply the toys, I will provide the transport.'

With that, she was gone.

I felt someone touch my shoulder and a business card was thrust into my hand by a senior civil servant in a black coat. 'Call me when you get back,' he said simply. 'I'll sort the transport.'

And that is precisely what I did when I flew home.

Again the response was overwhelming and very touching. One little girl turned up with her favourite toy dog and bear, to hand over to 'children much worse off than me'. In the end we collected seventeen tonnes of toys, from cuddly creatures of all sizes for small orphans to Take That pop memorabilia for the adolescents.

I stored them in Norwich Union's donated warehouse, where Scouts and Guides packed them over many long weekends.

One of the minister's twenty-tonne juggernauts turned up finally with a Croat lorry driver who took our load to the ODA warehouse in Illidza, on the outskirts of Sarajevo. The orphans were given their specially labelled boxes, designed to meet the needs of their different rooms and age groups.

The other toys were handed out to families from all sides in the conflict. After appeals were put out on local radio and television, mothers and fathers turned up with their children in their thousands and queued for many hours for the first new toy they had seen in years.

I knew we would not save anyone's life with such a gesture.

But with peace beginning to appear like a reality, it seemed right. If only to prove to children from across the city's great divides that there was still love in the world outside.

VII

NO-ONE KNEW HER REAL NAME,
SO THEY CALLED HER TENNEH

Freetown, Sierra Leone – May 1996

No-one knew her real name, so they called her Tenneh. It means 'God has provided,' which was appropriate for a six-year-old West African girl whose story of survival would enthral much of the developed world. She had been saved by one of those miracles of chance which can rekindle your faith in divine intervention.

Within all the accepted parameters of medical science and logic, she should have been dead. But, somehow, she had survived.

A heavy bullet from an automatic rifle had punched its way into her head and lodged behind her right eye. There it had remained, undetected, for over a year. The ugly, bleeding wound to the top of her head was thought to have been caused by a falling rock or the branch of a tree. It had been treated and healed up quickly.

Eventually, many months later, she had complained of headaches and problems with her vision and an X-ray had been taken of her skull.

The technician in the private scanning unit in Freetown, the teeming capital of Sierra Leone, could not believe his eyes. There on the black and white image was the unmistakable shape of the bullet, its point upper-most. The base was directly in line with her right nostril and the tip ended halfway up the eye socket on the same side.

'I could not believe what I was seeing,' he said later. 'I had never seen anything like this before in someone who was still alive. We had been expecting something completely different. No-one had expected this. It was hard to believe how she had survived.'

The world took a similar view. The story was dubbed 'The Miracle of Tenneh' and was covered by television, radio and press in almost every country across the globe during that incredible summer.

I became involved by sheer chance. Caroline Cook rang me from the Wiltshire home of Hope and Homes for Children with an extraordinary request.

'James, we have been approached by some people in Sierra Leone about a small girl who has a bullet in her brain and who needs an operation.

'I know you have carried out work with injured children from Bosnia and wondered what you thought about the chances. It seems an incredible stroke of luck that she has survived.'

There was no hesitation. What journalist would baulk at such a story? What father would not do all he could to give such a child another chance at life?

I took a note of what details Caroline knew and asked her to send me the crucial X-rays of the child's skull, together with her medical notes. In such cases, doctors will always demand such data to allow a prognosis to be made. Understandably, they are reluctant to become involved in so-called mercy airlifts of children if the chances of their survival are slim or negative. Clearly the death of such a child during treatment would be a humanitarian and public relations disaster for those concerned.

When the plates came, I could not believe their impact. They were clear and compelling images which would grace the front pages of the world's press. That was immediately obvious. What's more, the medical notes were thorough and accompanied by a statement from the man and wife who had found and cared for the injured girl. This was a survival story which would warm the hardest of hearts. It had to be told and Tenneh had to be helped, but in the best way possible.

I decided to take her case to my old friend Richard Drew at the Norfolk and Norwich Hospital. He had served a long military career, ultimately commanding a British Army Royal Electrical and Mechanical Engineer battalion in Germany, helping to keep tanks and other units ready to meet the Cold War threat from the Soviet Union. Now he was the hospital trust's administration director and had already played a major part in our airlift of Bosnian Admir Vele for an operation on his badly shot-up leg. He knew what bullets could do to the human body and was fascinated by the story.

'Leave it with me, James, I'll talk it through with the consultants and get back to you,' he promised.

Within days he was back and ready to make a firm offer.

'Bring her over to us and we'll have a look,' he said. 'We can't say what we can do until we perform our own tests, but we are happy to see her and, if possible, remove the bullet.'

That was the breakthrough. I told Mark and Caroline the good news and we began the complex planning of the airlift.

As with Admir, there would be a need to balance Tenneh's security and peace of mind with the publicity which would surround her. There would be the other hurdles of diplomacy and politics to cross. Mark, in particular, was concerned that Hope and Homes for Children did not wish to be portrayed as a charity which became involved in headline-grabbing publicity stunts. Its main objective was to provide long-term homes for children just like Tenneh, whose life had been disrupted by the death of her parents in her country's vicious civil war. We decided to ensure we had a thorough grasp of her story. We also needed to explain with unanimity that we were organising her airlift because of a cry for help from people who had nowhere else to turn.

Her story was recorded for us in the writings of Malomoh Cole, a bright young engineer who had found her alone and taken her to safety the previous year. Along with his wife, Mariama, he had been forced to escape the rebel gunmen who had been attempting to overthrow the government of Sierra Leone, one of the world's poorest countries. In a matter-of-fact style, his document related a trek to safety which became a bitter test of endurance in a land where killing, raping, looting and village burning were commonplace.

In his carefully worded statement, he told how Tenneh's story unfolded: 'It was on January 19 last year, in mid-morning, when the rebels attacked Moriba town and everyone took to their heels into the nearby bush.

'Mariama, who was heavily pregnant, and I, managed to walk nearly twenty-seven miles to the other villages where rebel attacks had not yet begun. Sporadic shooting forced us back into the bush to pass the night in a dilapidated farmhouse. No sooner had we reached the farmhouse, than I discovered a young child, crying, with no clothing and nobody to attend to her.

'I took her to the house and asked about her parents. But she was speechless with fear and appeared very hungry.

'Mariama prepared the small food we had and we all ate together. I therefore decided to name her Tenneh – meaning God has provided.

'Four days later we were back on the road to Mokanabogh village when we heard sporadic shooting which created pandemonium with everybody running to the bush.

'Myself, Mariama and Tenneh ran into nearby cover but, as it was getting dark, I left them to collect wood so that we could set it on fire for warmth and to keep the wild animals away.

'As soon as I had finished setting the fire, I suddenly saw Tenneh on the ground, shouting, with blood oozing from her head. She was unconscious for three hours.

'There were no drugs, but I had four packs of "pegapack" in my pocket.

I applied this medicine to the wound and the following day I had to carry her on my back to a nearby village since Mariama's feet were swollen. She later gave birth to a boy – our first born – who died soon after because of poor medical attention.

'Within five days, Tenneh's medical condition had deteriorated so much that I decided to surrender my life, together with Tenneh, to the rebels because they were the only people around the area with medical facilities.

'We went to the rebel base at Sierra Rutile mines hospital where I was tortured severely. Some rebels suggested killing me and Tenneh but, through the power of the Lord, they gave instructions to the nurse to give full-time treatment to Tenneh.

'We survived among the rebels for four days and I managed to escape with her when I thought she was a little improved.

'We joined Mariama in the bush and immediately took off and headed for Freetown in fear of frequent rebel patrols.

'We arrived in Freetown on April 27, three months and about 250 miles later, on foot, through the bush, carrying Tenneh and avoiding the rebels, in a very deplorable condition.

'There was nothing to live on, not even to support Tenneh's health. I had to plead for people to help her.

'We were lucky to get in touch with the social worker of the children's charity, Help a Needy Child International, a Mr Gblaa, who, on hearing of our plight, decided to register Tenneh as a HANCI child.

'On January 6 this year we took her to a Dr Willogby in Freetown who, on administering treatment, referred us to a clinic in Bathurst Street where the X-ray report showed a bullet in the atrium of her right eye.

'As a poor man I was worried about how to start tackling the problem. So we contacted the editor of the For Di People newspaper and showed him Tenneh's X-ray. He told us to write an article asking for assistance both locally and internationally to help save the life of this five-year-old girl.

'Thereafter Dr Roland Kargbo, of HANCI, contacted Hope and Homes for Children for assistance and every effort was started to save Tenneh.'

Medical reports suggested that Tenneh had suffered reduced vision in her right eye caused by the bullet damage and had also suffered some hearing and speech loss subsequently. This was believed to have been caused by follow-up infections, possibly Lassa fever transmitted through rats' urine, contracted when she lived, initially, with the Coles in the appalling Brickworks refugee camp in Freetown. The city was overwhelmed with displaced people, many of them having to live in such camps, where deaths from typhoid, cholera, meningitis and malaria were common.

With Malomoh's statement and the supporting medical reports to hand, we knew this was a genuine cry for help which could not be ignored.

It was evident that there would be criticism about plucking a child from Africa, treating her injuries and then sending her back. The answer was simply: 'What else would you have us do?' The alternatives were to leave her to her fate or to enable her to be adopted by a family in the UK. That would consign a traumatised child, with severe hearing and visual impairment, to life in a drastically alien culture and difficult climate. It would be an attractive proposition to a sentimentalist, but we knew that it would also be an insult to the people of Sierra Leone who were working so hard to provide care for children like Tenneh. At the time, we were helping Mark and Caroline to develop a £200,000 children's home in Makeni, a provincial town north-east of the capital, where Tenneh would be able to regain her life in the company of similar war orphans and caring staff who understood them.

In forthright terms, Mark summed up the difficulties: 'We were faced here with a terrible moral dilemma. The aim of our charity is to build homes and money is entrusted to us for that – so we could not use that to provide emergency treatment for Tenneh.

'We tried to get help for her from other charities in Sierra Leone, but no-one could do anything. So, when medical experts told us that the bullet in her head could eventually cause her death we agreed with our trustees that we would have to do everything possible.

'Tenneh is a symbol of the suffering of so many children. It is impossible to help every child, but how could we refuse her a chance? We just had to do something.'

HOPE and HOMES for Children

East Clyffe, Salisbury, Wiltshire. SP3 4LZ
Telephone: (01722) 790111 Fax: (01722) 790024
e-mail: hope_and_homes@dial.pipex.com
Web site: http://www.celtic-bear.com/hope/index.html
Registered Charity Number 1040534

A family and a future for young victims of war or disaster

INTERLUDE

NORWICH

We were able to beg and borrow many things. From air tickets to the medical work, people were quietly delighted to provide support when the story was related to them. At the hospital in Norwich, the irrepressible Richard Drew had paved the way for the treatment, some of which would be carried out by doctors in their own time. I talked in some depth with the man who would lead the medical team. Geoffrey Cheney was a charming surgeon with a quiet humour and a soft, comforting voice. A consultant oral and maxillo facial specialist, he had already become well used to rebuilding the faces of depressed farmers who had attempted suicide with shotguns – and failed. The grey-haired consultant had lived in Sierra Leone during his military service and had already begun to discuss Tenneh's case with doctors in his once-familiar Freetown.

He knew how lucky the youngster had been. It now appeared that she had been hit by a tumbling spent bullet, which had been fired into the air and fallen back to earth. Much of its deadly kinetic energy had already been dissipated as it struck the top of her head.

Geoffrey Cheney knew that the heavy round had ploughed through the right lobe of her brain before stopping. He knew that a movement just one millimetre forward would have caused her right eye to pop out. The same distance sideways would have pierced the optic nerve.

He was still 3,000 miles from his patient, but in his relaxed manner, he gave me his initial assessment: 'The bullet does lie perilously close to the optic nerve. Her vision and mobility of her right eye are reduced. That must have been caused first time round by the bullet. The round is lying within the cone of muscles attached to the eye and going through the middle is the optic nerve.

'Anything getting into there would have caused mayhem. But I am told she can move the eye, which is remarkable. The problem is the passage of time. This happened sixteen months ago and taking the bullet out may not actually make things any better because the damage done to the muscle has been replaced by fibrous scar tissue.

'What is even more remarkable is that she has any vision in that eye at all. I would have thought a bullet of that size would disrupt the nerve entirely.

124

Mark and Caroline Cook at the party for the rebuilt orphanage, Sarajevo 1995

Baroness Chalker and Mark Cook outside the rebuilt orphanage

Mark Cook with orphans, Sierra Leone 1996

Tenneh Cole in Brickworks Refugee Camp, Sierra Leone 1996

The author with the Makeni orphans, Sierra Leone 1996

School children in Freetown, Books Appeal 1998

Moving to the new orphanage, Makeni 1996

The new orphanage completed

'The oddest thing is that the bullet is sitting there and appears to have done remarkably little damage. It has gone through her head, presumably from the top, and right the way down and lodged itself.

'You can lose quite a lot of brain without any noticeable difficulties. Large areas of brain do something, but nobody knows quite what.'

The senior surgeon knew there would be a great deal of pressure to remove the bullet. But he was adamant that his team would do only what was in Tenneh's best interests. I concurred entirely with that view. As a journalist, I could already see how the bullet would become an icon, to be extracted and shown to the watching TV and Press cameras like some sacrificial offering. They needed this tangible symbol of the virility of our developed world, not some fudge with doctors telling them that the bullet was best left alone. But that demand would be resisted, if it became necessary to do so.

The judgement would be taken among the Cheney team. This included an ear, nose and throat surgeon who would investigate Tenneh's deafness and speech problems. A neuro-surgeon would look at the extent of brain damage and the potential for removing the bullet. And an ophthalmic specialist would consider the best interests of her sight. Among their tests would be CT scanning to provide a three-dimensional computer image of the brain. The hospitals' Magnetic Resonance Imaging scanner could not be used because of the dangers of its magnetic field moving the metal bullet with dire consequences for the patient.

We were given the all-clear to fly out in early May and bring Tenneh to the UK. Mark and Caroline had been to Sierra Leone before. To me it had been a distant former British colony, known only through A-level geography lessons for Freetown's magnificent deep-water port, one of the finest in Africa and a regular stopping-off point for ships plying the Cape route. Mark, who had travelled the world with the Gurkhas, had been mesmerised by his first visit to one of the world's poorest countries.

I, too, was to find myself falling into the pit of its treacherous beauty, to the point where I was virtually consumed by its hidden horrors.

The three of us eventually joined the early morning Sabena flight from Heathrow to Brussels and on to Freetown, feeling trepidation and a certain satisfaction. Our logistics appeared to have worked smoothly. Despite the enormity of the story as a journalistic scoop, it had remained under wraps until the front page of that day's *Eastern Daily Press* had announced the details to what was to become a waiting world. When you work for a regional newspaper you know your community and take a certain pride in giving them an exclusive. I had prepared three days of features which would reveal the whole Tenneh saga, from the staggering X-ray picture and Malomoh's epic trek on day one to the medical assessment of her case.

125

Interlude

The national Press and television, with their huge resources, open cheque books and, sometimes, dubious methods, would be left chasing the story until our return. Even that had been catered for. Mark retained the services of a public relations agency, run by Mike Dewar, an old Army friend, who would manage the media coverage and the Heathrow press conference a week later.

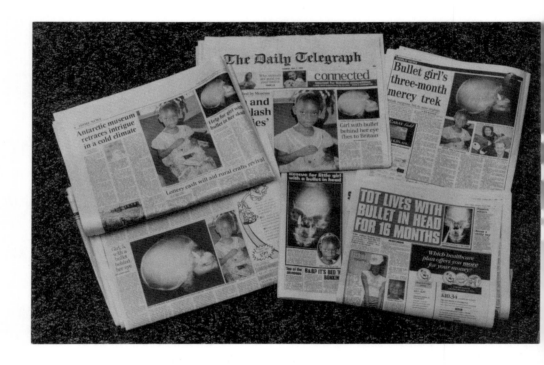

VIII

AMBUSH ALLEY

Freetown, Sierra Leone – 1996

After a long, packed and tiring flight, the Airbus touched down at Freetown's Lungi International airport in a heat haze. Mark had warned me of the culture shock from his previous trips there. I had travelled widely and was shocked by few places. But this was different.

Lungi was set on the edge of a peninsula across the huge bay on which Freetown stands. To journey from the airport to the city involves a tortuous taxi trip to a ramshackle ferry and a voyage of an hour or more across the water. The alternative is a $60 US flight on an old Russian helicopter which we had been advised against.

First, though, the airport terminal had to be penetrated.

Few places on earth can witness such frenetic activity as the arrivals lounge at Lungi when the 'big bird' from Brussels has arrived. After the usual round of threats and demands from various uniformed and plain-clothes officials, you find yourself bounced into a heaving mass of soldiers, policemen and locals all desperate to make a fast buck out of you and your vulnerability.

Luckily, we had a vehicle waiting from HANCI, driven by the formidable Abu, a muscular and unflappable character whose constant smile belies his composure and reliability in a tight corner. Security trained, he was a one-time driver on the staff of a past British High Commissioner until a newcomer in the post sacked him and twenty-three other staff. 'He did not like black men, so we all had to go,' he once told me. 'Then he replaced us all with more black men.'

Abu soon had us and our bags loaded onto his Toyota pick-up and we were heading for the ferry. After travelling for twenty hours non-stop, there was an immediate shock in leaving the fly-by-wire technology of Sabena's Airbus and finding yourself plunged into a midnight ferry queue that included goats, chickens and a collection of humanity who appeared to be clinging to survival by their fingertips. Children on crutches, with one arm or leg, begged for coins alongside old blind men. Women, their heads supporting huge bags of fruit or old clothes, attempted to jump from the landing onto the bouncing ramp as the ageing steel ship prepared to sail.

The bay was choppy and the ship awash with people, animals and vehicles. In a West African country which has slumped to one of the three poorest in the world, this link with the city was an economic lifeline for many people. They had to sell their possessions or products there or their families would not eat. That was the reality. The journey was arduous, but not as difficult as another ferry which had sailed that night from Freetown to Conakry in neighbouring Guinea. We discovered later that it had sunk in the rough conditions and over 300 people were drowned.

As we came closer to Freetown in the blackness of the night, its thousands of flickering oil lamps took shape on the horizon, along with the small sections lit by its single power plant. At Government wharf, the mass of four-and-two-legged passengers poured down the ramp and we were taken to the Paramount Hotel. Mark had warned me that its name suggested more than was on offer. The green and yellow edifice had seen better times. So too had the good time girls who eyed us in the lobby, including one we were told was known as 'Snowdrop', a dramatically constructed woman whose white trouser suit appeared to have been fitted with the use of a pneumatic pump.

Upstairs, my single room was stifling due to an ancient air-conditioning unit. In the early dawn, the view included the flat-roofed restaurant where ugly, grey vultures were padding around in anxious anticipation. Sleep was difficult in a bed with a sagging mattress, which appeared to have been frequented by the gigantic Snowdrop on more than one occasion.

Next morning, though, Mark and Caroline were at their best. Thirty years travelling the world with the Army had taught them not to suffer shortcomings in service with quiet stoicism. They had organised the restaurant staff into bringing the right tea, fruit and toast in the correct quantities, and precisely when we required them.

Over the coming days, such assertiveness was to prove invaluable. Six years of civil war against revolutionary guerrillas had battered the friendly and industrious people of this one-time paradise into virtual submission. Thousands had been killed, maimed and made homeless by the terror attacks in the countryside. The economy had been devastated, with one of the few continuing enterprises being the heavily corrupt mining of the fabulously-rich diamond reserves. The result was a kind of inertia and desperation among many people whose only hope was that their first democratically elected president, Ahmed Tejan Kabbah, would lead them out of their pit of sorrows. Many did not seem to be holding their breath in anticipation.

As we headed north to the children's home in Makeni, the devastation in the countryside became frighteningly obvious. Every few kilometres, we came across the remnants of a once idyllic village, the thatched huts now blackened, burned-out ruins, their people either dead or fled. We stopped regularly at checkpoints where wary Sierra Leone soldiers were surprised to see three white people heading along a road that had been regularly ambushed. Indeed, one section was known as Ambush Alley. A straight run with high sandy banks on either side, it was a perfect position to set up a road block and pour fire into trapped vehicles from the high ground.

Poignantly, we passed the burned-out trucks there and the overgrown crosses which marked the graves of peacekeeping soldiers from Guinea who had been wiped out in just such an ambush.

It was a baking late afternoon when we were greeted by the Makeni sign erected by the town's Rotary club. It proved a graphic contrast to Freetown's sewer-crossed shanties and decaying colonial buildings. This was a pleasant, spacious provincial town, with attractive wooden homes set along brown dirt roads and with a welcoming aura. The town centre boasted a colourful market and a Barclays Bank, run by a Mr Smith and a Mr Jones.

It was when we swung north and headed to the outlying streets that we found what we had come for. The sounds of the children's voices drifted through the truck's open windows:

> *'Welcome everyone to the house of peace and love,*
> *Welcome everyone to our home ...'*

It was a sound which was to become familiar over the coming days and months: the voices of orphans who had lost everything greeting those who had come from afar to offer them affection and some security.

As the pick-up slowed, they were gathered in the dusty roadway, clapping, singing, smiling, being urged on by a big man, with a round face, who was beaming with a gigantic smile. This was the wonderful Joseph Kargbo, their 'Uncle Joseph', the man who was to become a great friend and whom I was to christen 'Harry' for his Harry Belafonte-style charm and voice.

And there, too, at the front of the children, clapping and mouthing words to the song was Tenneh, 'the miracle girl' I recognised from photographs. She was tall for a six-year-old and had those two enormous brown eyes that would soon mesmerise the world. It was difficult to believe that behind that right eye sat that ugly Kalashnikov bullet that could easily have taken her life.

As we stepped down, the orphans broke ranks, still singing, and mobbed us, their small hands grabbing ours and pulling at our clothes. Some jumped in delight at being visited.

Over the next two days, Joseph, the deputy home manager, showed us round the cramped single-storey building that housed forty-four children who had lost their parents, their natural homes and all contact with supporting relatives. They slept on bunks, six to a room, and ate communally in the dusty back yard of the wooden building. All became individuals as the hours wore on. There was sad-faced Fatama who had been abducted and treated unspeakably by rebels, before being released to find her parents had been tortured and beheaded. Or there was smaller and quieter Fatima whose mother died when her bus was sprayed with bullets. Her mother was followed soon after by her father, who suffered a fatal stroke, leaving the seven-year-old alone for two weeks until aid workers found her. The stories were all a litany of man's cruelty to the innocent.

But there was kindness from the big man with the gentle voice and ready smile. That first day he had organised a wonderful meal of meat, peppers, spices, vegetables and casava, a favourite Sierra Leone leaf and very like spring cabbage, and he told me of the hurdles that lay ahead, in his calm and eloquent tone.

'The children have been given back some stability, but they need more love and care than we can give here. They really need individual attention because they have experienced such terror in their lives.

'Some have seen their mothers and fathers killed in front of them. Then they have had to flee for their lives, living in the bush for weeks or months, eating berries and leaves, drinking from streams, always watching for the rebels.

'For some, the next stop was a displacement camp. In Freetown, they have encountered shortages of food and water and terrible disease, seeing their friends die. It will take years to put that behind them, years of love and kindness. That is what they need.

'And Tenneh is one of them, only she has an added burden, a bullet in her head and trouble with her hearing, her right eye and her speech. She will need extra care to see her through. Care and love.

'The new home will be a great boost to them, a new start. It will show that they have a platform for the future, provided by you, the people who can give them the stability that has been snatched from their young lives.'

That night the children giggled themselves to sleep as they thought of their visitors. Next day, we visited the site of the £200,000 new home which Mark and Caroline were creating about two kilometres south.

Tenneh came with us in the pick-up along with her special friend, Amie Jabatti, a cute and lively terrier of a six-year-old. Amie's village was caught in crossfire between rebels and government forces. When it ended, her parents had been beheaded and she had been carried to a camp by her grandmother, who also soon died. United by tragedy, however, the two friends were inseparable. Tenneh would use hand signals and attempt to mouth words, sometimes lashing out in frustration. Amie would just laugh and tickle her.

Along with our truck-full of orphans, Mark and Caroline were delighted at the progress of the work since their last visit. In a compound the size of two soccer pitches, men were beavering away in 47° Centigrade searing heat, digging three deep wells, building walls for the pretty bungalows and making a communal, thatched roundhouse meeting area in traditional style in the centre of the site. It was an impressive project, notably for its intimacy. Every bungalow would accommodate just eight children, each with a house aunt to provide close care and affection. Maybe even love.

'It's amazing how quickly they're working,' enthused Mark. 'It's being built in a pretty, rural area where there's plenty of room to play and to create their own garden. Most of them come from rural areas and they love gardening. It's part of life here.

'There will also be animals here, pigeons, ducks, a couple of pet dogs, so it should be like a scene from the "good life".'

Next morning we packed to leave with Tenneh. I took a last look round the old home. In the garden I was shown the children's vegetable plot, sprouting with such delights as cashews and sweet potatoes. Ibrahim, short, fat and one of the youngest toddlers, showed me why they were thriving by urinating on several of the plants, shouting with delight as he ran off.

Nearby, though, was a reminder of the psychological scars these children carried with them. On a previous trip Mark had brought a soft toy for each of them. Very few were still in evidence in the bedrooms. But I spotted a few near the vegetable plot. They had had their insides torn out and had been buried in the brown soil. 'They are dead now,' one small boy, Farki told me, 'just dead.'

Tenneh cried as she left with us in the pickup. Amie cried too and stamped her feet in the dusty street until we were gone from sight. Accompanying us was HANCI aid worker Henry Abu, who had had some nursing training and was to act as interpreter and chaperone throughout her visit to England. It was a poor choice, largely because Henry was disliked instantly by Tenneh. It soon became clear that she was a determined and self-willed child. How else would she have survived her ordeal? And she would refuse to accept anything or anyone she did not like. Henry also appeared to misinterpret his role. Clearly it was a dream for an impoverished young man from Freetown to be whisked to England for a high profile visit. It was likely he would want to make the best of it. But the investment was being made to assist Tenneh, not Henry. It soon became obvious that he required clarification on this point. On the ferry to Lungi airport, Mark called upon his senior Army officer skills to 'brief' Henry on his crucial role. We knew the eyes of the world would be upon the two of them.

We also knew the next few days – even weeks – would be filled with trauma for her. But I hoped the excitement might temper the fear.

As we waited at a heaving Lungi for the Sabena flight, I bought a bangle and torch for Tenneh, who played with Caroline's toiletries, covering her face with tinted face powder. I wondered if she was simply being a child. She repeated the exercise during the flight and it seemed she was attempting to mimic the three of us, as we were almost certainly the first white faces she had seen. Jetting along above the Atlantic Ocean held no horrors for her, as she ate extra desserts and starters from our in-flight meals.

At Brussels, Sabena, which had provided free seats for Tenneh and Henry, fast-tracked us through to the shuttle to London.

But at Heathrow, we were immersed in a media scrum and a truly international press conference which beamed pictures and copy round the world. As expected, the role of the *Eastern Daily Press* was removed from most reports, although I was asked some particularly tricky medical questions due to the fact there was no-one else present who was suitably qualified to answer them. Mark and Caroline gave sterling performances. Henry spoke with astounding sensitivity about Tenneh, who simply played with a yellow Hope and Homes balloon.

Outside, Mark and Caroline bade us farewell as they headed home to Salisbury. I noticed Tenneh was now gripping my hand continually, instead of Henry's, as we picked up my car and made for Norwich.

I had arranged for some toys and food to be available for the journey. Tenneh was excited and lively, pointing and laughing at some of the sights she was seeing. If she was communicating with Henry, he was not prepared to say much. I wondered if he was reacting against Tenneh's rejection of him, or even against Mark's lecture. I was beginning to wonder if a power struggle was developing between patient and chaperone, with me caught in the middle.

As we wheeled through the front gates of the Norfolk and Norwich Hospital, the television crews on the lawn spotted us immediately and began to film. Richard Drew, army trained and alert, was quick to shepherd the three of us into a private room. He had arranged a sequence of TV and stills filming with Tenneh to satisfy the media temporarily. She was then to be allowed to settle in and recover in the caring hands of her regular nurses, Helen Shorten and Teresa Richardson. Henry and I were steered toward a press conference with the Cheney team. The most memorable question came from a freelance journalist who, when told that the bullet in Tenneh's head had the potential of a ticking timebomb, asked: 'When is it expected to explode?'

Later I took Henry to Superdrug for some toiletries, fitting in a Sky News interview on the hospital lawn on the way back. I had already briefed Richard on my concerns about Henry's role and left him, with spending money and comfortably ensconced in a hospital apartment, where he had access to a telephone, television lounge, kitchen and regular meals from the restaurant.

After filing my copy and twelve films of stills at the office, I arrived home before midnight for a very late family reunion. Next morning at 7 a.m., the telephone rang. It was Henry: 'James. I have not got a comb. Can you get me one this morning?'

After almost two days without sleep, it was like waking up to a surreal nightmare.

'A what?' I blurted.

'A comb. You did not get me one yesterday and I must have one.'

'OK, Henry, your wish is my command,' I said ironically, put the phone down and went back to sleep.

I knew Henry took almost fastidious care with his appearance. But, in the scale of what was happening, his comb became a great leveller. Here I was, caught up in a mercy mission to provide a young orphan with the chance of an operation to remove a bullet from her brain. It was on every front page in Europe and further afield. Truly, the eyes of the world were watching.

And I was being asked to go shopping for a comb for the man who was supposed to be providing support for her. I bought the comb at a local newsagent and delivered it to Henry, as requested. I also visited Tenneh and Richard. She was settling in well, helping the nurses with cleaning and whatever she could on the friendly Laura Stuart children's ward.

As the days passed, her confidence grew. The Cheney team continued their careful assessments of her problems and, particularly, the bullet. Donations were also pouring in for a special trust fund we had announced for her future medical treatment and education.

Then, four days after her arrival, Geoffrey Cheney announced he would go ahead and extract the rifle round.

Doctors had decided that the risk of infection from the bullet was greater than the risk of the three-hour operation. He pointed out: 'The tests show there is no sight in her right eye, but there is potential for infection and if we are ever to get her eye, which has diverged, back into alignment with her good eye, we have to get the bullet out.

'It's easy enough to remove it, but the danger lies in causing more mayhem in doing so. And she's got quite enough damage as it is.

'We shall be working on a very small scale. At the moment I am keeping my cards close to my chest about how I shall remove it. We will have to see what we find when we start – but I might at the end of the day, try to cut the bullet in half with a small drill to get it out.'

He was to be assisted by a fellow consultant oral and maxillo facial surgeon, as well as an anaesthetist from Great Ormond Street Children's Hospital in London and planned an approach from two directions – the mouth and the front of the face.

He also felt certain the operation would not bother Tenneh, whom he described as 'totally relaxed'.

'I don't think it will upset her too much. She will have a bit of a fat face for a while and a little scar beneath the eye.'

When it happened, the operation went very smoothly. The whole bullet was extracted and a special titanium clamp fitted to bridge the space created beneath the eye. Tenneh recovered rapidly and was soon helping Helen and the other nurses in their ward duties. She had a predisposition for nursing sick children, possibly something she had experienced during her time in the refugee camps of Freetown.

Meanwhile, I managed to keep Henry busy on a round of activities. Tenneh had frozen him out completely by now, sometimes turning noisily aggressive at his approach.

He was hard to contact at times. Hospital staff sometimes complained they could not find him when he was needed to interpret during tests on Tenneh's hearing and recovery process. In audiology, so difficult was the translation problem that staff used another interpreter at one point.

And then Henry took a trip to the Midlands, where he told me he was 'making contacts' and was out of touch with the hospital and me.

There was no doubt, however, that everything else was going to plan.

Tenneh's story had travelled across the world. Geoffrey had received calls from friends and relatives who had seen him on their television screens as far afield as Australia, Hong Kong and the United States. Truly she was *the* girl of hope that summer. But there was still a need for her to return home when she was well. Psychologists felt that was the best course for her. Some people had offered to adopt her and give her a new life in England. One woman was even threatening to take out a court order to prevent her from leaving the country. But there was no doubt that this small girl was traumatised by being in such an exotic land and culture, without the support of her friends and the familiar things she had known from birth. Behind the smiling pictures so beloved of the media, were those gloomy times when she would appear desperately homesick and fractious. On top of those considerations, it would have been an insult to the people of Sierra Leone as well as our own partners there, not to allow them to look after her future in her new home. The civil war was still raging and there was abject poverty, but it would have been immoral to have brought her to England for surgery and to have broken our word by keeping her here permanently.

Mark and Caroline were equally adamant that it would have been wrong for Tenneh and for the charity to remove her from her homeland as a token orphan. We had given her a new chance at life. Now we were taking her back to a new home.

When the time came for her return, they were devastated that they had to represent Hope and Homes for Children at a major international conference, instead of travelling back to Freetown. I booked the flights and hatched a plan that would reduce the trauma for her. Henry had become unpredictable. I did not know what his next move might be, so I decided to opt for a rapid departure. I told him he and Tenneh would be coming to spend a few days with my family and me. A final press conference was held. Tenneh had been fitted with a powerful Dannavox hearing aid, which she would need to be convinced to wear. And I picked up Henry.

He appeared at his apartment with piles of clothes, shoes and a huge box containing a television set. I told him we would be lucky to get the set onto the aircraft, even with Sabena's magnanimous assistance.

There was sadness among the nurses when Tenneh finally said goodbye. Helen Shorten, in particular, had been attached to her and had mothered her. She spoke for all of them: 'She's a very lovable little girl, she's made friends with everyone – and it's going to be very quiet without her.'

In fact, the chocolate-loving girl from Africa did not really want to leave the district general hospital. In the end, a nurse had to join us for part of the journey, as Tenneh sat in the middle of the rear seat, alongside Henry in my car, sobbing miserably.

She settled in quickly during her day and night at our home in the countryside near Norwich, playing with Janna's dolls. Only once did she show her anxiety or frustration when she lashed out at Jared, giving him a shiner on his left eye.

Next day, I informed a stunned Henry we were leaving for the airport and packed the car with his bags, together with as many of Tenneh's toys and other gifts as I hoped we could carry. His television had to be repacked into a smaller box. Then we were off.

Mark met us at Heathrow where there was another international press conference to register the departure of the 'miracle girl'. After an hour under the hot TV lights, Tenneh was coping quite well, smiling and playing with her toys. But I decided she had had enough as she faced a long journey. As I took her to the departure area, she began to cry due to the exhaustion and stress. The cameras began to flash at that point and some newspapers decided to use that picture as an illustration of an unhappy Tenneh being sent home. That could not have been further from the truth, as was recorded by a BBC East film crew who I invited to join us for the trip back to Sierra Leone.

Sabena were very accommodating once more, even allowing Henry's television into the hold at no extra charge. And Tenneh brightened as we took off, enjoying everything the airline caterers could throw at her.

In Freetown, the whole mission appeared to have become a national symbol of hope. At a televised press conference soon after our arrival, I thanked everyone concerned for their help in giving her a new chance of life. The only downside to the whole day was Henry. He came to me complaining that he had just unwrapped the television set and the screen was broken. I wondered if he had the proper perspective on what had happened. But then I lived in a comfortable home in a rich country. And I had a functioning television set.

The next day proved just how right we had been to take her home. With Abu driving us in the pick-up out of the capital, Tenneh hugged a cold bottle of Pierval spring water to her chest in the dripping heat. As the truck swung left into a narrow entrance, she murmured in Krio and a smile as big as an African moon burst across her face, the first in a long while. She had recognised the home of Malomoh Cole, the man who had saved her life and given her her name. And she was happy. She hugged him and his wife Mariama as we met outside the first-floor apartment where she stayed with them that night.

In the morning we picked her up to take her the 180 kilometres north to Makeni and to her friends at the children's home. Malomoh and Mariama had already conceded that they would never be able to afford to give her accommodation and, reluctantly, had let her go to grow up with the other HANCI orphans.

The journey was less tense because of the ceasefire which had followed the recent elections. It was incongruous to note the smiling faces of one group of young soldiers at a checkpoint adorned with the leg bone and skull of a rebel fighter they had killed.

As the Makeni home came into view, once again we heard those rich young voices. It emerged that the children had been awaiting our arrival for four hours in baking sun, but they were still able to project that joyous melody:

'Welcome Sister Tenneh to the house of peace and love.'

A tear came to my eye when they and Uncle Joseph spotted me and they switched the words immediately to:

'Welcome brother James to the house of peace and love.'

Tenneh leapt down and was reunited with a hug from Amie, still her special friend. They immediately dived into the garden to play with her new toys.

Later, in the wilting heat, I enrolled Tenneh at the nearby St Joseph's School for Hearing Impaired Children, one of only two specialist schools in the whole country. Run by Roman Catholic Cluny sisters, the large white and airy building provided an education for 164 children with hearing problems. It gave them vocational training to enable them to earn a living and prepared the academically gifted to use hearing aids and to transfer to ordinary schools.

Tenneh, we were told by English-trained hearing instructor Andrew Kamara, would be taught to use the Dannavox aid I had brought from England. Echoing suspicions voiced already by doctors in England, he said she may have been pretending not to have been able to hear anything through natural caution and reticence. This point had been further confirmed by tests I had conducted the previous day at the British Clinic in Freetown. There she had refused to acknowledge any sound until she giggled after being told a joke in Krio.

As Tenneh ran with delight through the school's long corridors, pursued by a screaming Amie, it was clear that the pieces of the jigsaw of her restored young life were falling, miraculously, into place.

The trust fund had reached £16,000 to provide her with some security and future help, and she would be taught by Irish nuns at a school which understood her particular difficulties. On top of that, the new home would be open in three months. It included a building dedicated as the *Eastern Daily Press* library and, foolishly, perhaps, I pledged that I would fill it with books for the children eventually.

When the time came to leave, I gave Tenneh a hug and she laughed. But there was no sorrow at my parting. I was a reminder of a strange time. It might have been exciting. But now she was back with her friends. Among them, Amie appeared the most sorrowful. She was often the last to step forward and the last to let go, shy but determined.

And Joseph, my Harry Belafonte, also gave me a hug with one of his intuitive comments: 'We cannot thank you enough for what you have done, except to say you must come back. That is what these children need and treasure most, the people who come back.' Little did I know how little time was left for the man I had come to know as a friend, the children's Uncle Joseph, a truly gentle giant.

As I flew home with the BBC team at the end of the week, I reflected on a mission that had been filled with raw emotion and had always been balanced on the fine edge of success and disaster. In the end, the result had been more than anyone could have prayed for three long months earlier.

There were many tribulations ahead. But for the moment I could not avoid the simple thought about what had happened.

This had been Tenneh Cole. Miracle girl. Starting life again. Thank-you.

IX

THE ORPHANS LEFT IN THE NIGHT

Freetown, Sierra Leone – December 1998

The orphans left in the night. Some were crying. Others were passive, carefully carrying their few possessions in brightly coloured rucksacks. All were uncertain what the future would hold for them.

Once again.

This time, the killers had come with a warning. They were the survivors of the rebel junta which had been in charge for many months until they had been blasted out of the Capital, Freetown, by an invasion led by Nigerian peacekeepers. It had taken them several days to travel the 180 kilometres north to Makeni, where the children's home was based.

But they had arrived finally. Now they were killing, maiming and raping at random in the town. Houses and shops were on fire and shooting filled the night sky.

It would not be long before they turned their evil on the home and, possibly, the children. So it was decided to flee into the bush, whatever that might mean.

The home manager, Peter Brymer, knew the bush well. He shepherded the sixty children, some as young as three, to a sacred Bundu site where female circumcisions were conducted. It was somewhere, he felt, that even the rebels would not dare to desecrate.

For Tenneh Cole, Amie Jabatti, Hassana Koromoa and many others, the nightmare had come back. They had lost their parents and their natural homes in similar atrocities. Now the terror had returned to haunt them.

And this was terror of the deepest magnitude.

During their time in control of Freetown, the drug-crazed rebel followers, including long-serving bush fighters and newly-acquired defectors from the national Army, had committed appalling crimes.

In animist rituals they had torn the hearts out of opponents, shown them to the victims whilst still attached to their body, and then severed their arteries. Sons had been decapitated and their mothers forced to breast feed the severed heads. And children had had their hands, arms and legs cut off and eyes gouged out as 'terror envoys' to be sent to those who might challenge their rule.

Now that their period of power had come to a bloody end, they were seeking revenge. Many people had fled the quiet provincial town of Makeni as they had raped and murdered their way north.

Now it was time for the children to flee too.

For three long weeks, they clung to life in the bush, begging food and water from generous villagers, eating leaves and berries and taking shelter in an abandoned building far from any dangerous road or track used by the marauding killers.

By the time the Nigerian Alpha jets finally dropped their bombs on the rebels and the ground forces followed on, the orphans had suffered a living hell. Many had acquired skin diseases, stomach disorders and psychological problems. They had seen neighbouring children die from snake bites. But they were all still alive and that was thanks to the skill of their guardians.

When they returned to the home it had been devastated. The walls still stood, but everything had been looted: pots, pans, mattresses, toys, books, even their all-important house-slippers. The process of restoration began.

The *Eastern Daily Press* asked readers for help and, almost overnight, £6,000 came in. The money was used by Mark and Caroline Cook to buy essentials immediately. Bedding, clothes, cooking equipment, even hair-brushes were bought to give the children back some sense of normality and dignity.

But it would never be the same. It had been almost two years since I had taken Tenneh back from her operation in England. I had returned later, alone, that year for the opening of the spacious new complex. There had been such joy as the children had danced and sung and played football with me in their big compound.

Tenneh had played with the counting set and Little Ibrahim had driven crazily around in the red and yellow plastic buggy which I had brought with me from England.

Their Uncle Joseph had been delighted and had also given me his traditional bear hugs during the week I spent with them. He had also afforded me a special privilege, taking me one rainy night in the truck into the deepest bush. With lightning streaking above the tall palms, we had parked and then walked a kilometre along a trail to a collection of huts, lit by the flashes and my small torch. There we had met two men dressed in loin cloths. I was asked to sit on a log with them and they poured a liquid from a large urn into a plastic cup. This was the sacred local palm wine and these

Emma Williams, Freetown 1998

'Uncle Joseph' Kargbo at the Makeni orphanage, 1996

The author with Tenneh and her rescuers, the Coles, Sierra Leone 1996

Machete victim, Korie Samara, and his sisters, Sierra Leone 1998

Construction of the orphanage, Makeni 1996

Adrian Horn with local police, Freetown 1998

Tenneh with friends outside the *EDP* Library, Makeni 1996

were its makers. In a jungle clearing, in the middle of a rainy season storm I was sitting close to the hamlet which was the home of one of the rebel leaders, drinking what Joseph described as 'the finest palm wine in Africa'. No white man had ever been there. Nor was one ever likely to go there again. It was an honour I would savour forever.

We had laughed and joked like long-lost friends that night as Joseph and I became saturated in the warm and teeming rain. The wine was gently alcoholic and tasted dry, natural and thirst-quenching. It was to be the last time I would see him this way. When I left the following day, he issued one of his bear-hug-and-handslap goodbyes. And I was gone.

So too was he just over a year later, killed in the Nigerian invasion of Freetown. He had gone there to arrange supplies for the home when the shelling had started from naval ships in the bay. Hit in the shoulder by shrapnel, he had tried to escape on an overloaded ferry which had been swamped soon after leaving port. Injured and unable to swim, he had slid into the warm Atlantic water and drowned with scores of others. The end of a truly gentle giant.

Peter Brymer who had shepherded the children during their ordeal was a different style of manager. Strict and formidable, he was very capable and resourceful in times of crisis. But no-one could replace the gentle giant the children had known and loved so well.

On their return, they set about tidying their bungalows and eating areas. Rubbish was strewn everywhere, as the rebels had ransacked and destroyed what they could not carry. The children even took time to clean up the damaged tributes which had been created in the home. Some were dedicated to people who had constructed buildings. One in particular was the source of huge embarrassment and pride to me. In the centre of the site were two huge granite outcrops which had been impossible to remove. They had been turned into features. One had been named after Mark and Caroline Cook. The other had a white stone fixed to it bearing the simple black words, RUDDY'S HEIGHTS.

I often wondered if I truly deserved to have a little piece of Africa named after me.

Mark visited the home soon after the children returned. He told me: 'The children appeared to be fine but it is impossible to tell how they have been affected by the trauma of their escape from the rebels.'

And Tenneh too was reported to be in fine health. BBC journalist Dominic Medley explained: 'She was remarkable compared to the last time I saw her a year ago. She was very affectionate, very lively, speaking a few words, dancing, clapping and bigger now. She seemed like a young little seven-year-old girl and was far more lively.'

Her friend Amie Jabatti had been fostered by a local mission worker and his family. When Mark had visited her, she had appeared fearful that he had come to take her away. She recovered her composure when she was told he was just visiting her new-found family, the first since her natural parents had been slaughtered.

It seemed remarkable that children who had suffered so much could recover so well.

Locked in their young minds were horrors which few of us could imagine. Yet they were coping and appeared to be thriving.

It was then that I decided to fulfil my pledge to stock their *Eastern Daily Press* library with books. I had recovered from my own personal trauma: four days in the Norfolk and Norwich Hospital suffering from malaria.

On my lone trip to record the opening of the new home, I had been unable to take the most potent anti-malarials due to the side effects. The cover I had opted for had not been good enough and I was bitten on the right temple by a huge mosquito which had come out of the swamps during an overnight stay I had made at Lakka, near Freetown. The resulting fever had been of classic intensity. I was told it could have killed me within forty-eight hours. It had been a salutary lesson. But then I had always told myself that crossing the road can be fatal too.

So I decided I was ready to return. This time with a symbol of the future, twenty tonnes of books to create the new library for the children and to rebuild schools ransacked by the rebels.

After just three weeks of low key publicity, *Eastern Daily Press* readers hit the target amount. It was an impressive load, thousands of boxes filled with good books, rulers, pens, pencils, erasers, geometry sets, files, paper and exercise books. Norfolk Guides and a range of local companies and had also rallied round: warehousing, transport, packing and administration were all dealt with. As well as the storage and distribution some people also gave money to help with the shipping of our big steel container from Felixstowe.

When I flew into Sierra Leone, it was a very different place from two years previously. The flight was to Conakry, the capital of neighbouring Guinea, followed by a small plane ride down the coast and inland to the tiny Hastings airstrip, a few miles north of Freetown. The rebels were just thirty miles down the road, mounting increasingly successful and bold attacks against the Nigerian, Ecomog, strongpoints. The error committed earlier in the year when the rebels had been removed from Freetown was that they had not been pursued and wiped out. They had regrouped and were now an estimated 8,000-strong, attacking on at least three fronts, supported by the rich diamond fields which they were exploiting. Freetown was in some panic the week I arrived. The onset of the dry season in November gave the rebels the upper hand, allowing greater mobility through the bush, where the Nigerians were on unequal terms and refused to be drawn.

Despite this, the books had arrived and were safely locked in a secure warehouse in Freetown's port district known as Kissy Mess Mess. Not only that, Tenneh had arrived from Makeni for a medical examination just before a major rebel attack led to the road north being cut off.

When we met again after two years, it was in a teeming street in the heart of a capital city bursting with frightened refugees. I walked up to her. She was unsmiling and looked troubled. I held out a hand. She took it and said something that sounded like 'Kush, porto' ('Hello, white man). I had not expected more from a girl who might, rightfully, have hoped to have seen the back of the pale-faced man who had caused such trauma for her.

We walked to a nearby street stall where I asked her which Christmas present she wanted. She rejected a pink elephant and red dog in favour of a small cream rabbit. She was adamant and forceful about her decision. Tenneh Cole, I concluded, had not lost her legendary spirit of determination.

Over the coming days, I took her with HANCI's representatives to the televised presentation of the container and to donations of truckloads of the books. Dozens of schools which had almost nothing were able to take advantage of our donations.

On one trip, we journeyed thirty kilometres from town into the bush along the Lungi peninsula where the villages and schools had suffered the worst. It was the road taken by the retreating rebels earlier in the year and they had delivered vengeance on the innocent fishing and farming communities who scraped a living there.

Everywhere the Nigerian troops manning the roadblocks looked jumpy. The rebels had learned that the peacekeepers were stretched along the main roads. If they attacked in sufficient numbers they could wipe out such posts, killing everyone and creating fear. The peninsula was known to be a rebel operations base. And the soldiers appeared surprised to see a white man passing through. The price on my head was around £20,000, a figure established by the abduction of an Italian priest the previous week. He was on offer in exchange for a £15,000 satellite telephone and a £5,000 consignment of drugs.

Abu was taking no chances, particularly with heavy machine guns and blowpipe anti-armour missiles being aimed at his windscreen at some of the better armed barriers.

When he finally pulled the Toyota Hi-Lux into the forecourt of the Russell Sattia school a familiar sound filled the steaming air.

'While shepherds watched their flocks by night, all seated on the ground...'

It had a strange resonance in the burning heat and shirt-sticking humidity. Then the children's voices changed as they became aware of our presence.

Out they spilled in yellow shirts and brown shorts, excited, with their headmaster at the front.

When I told him we had come from England with a truck filled with books for his children, he said he did not have one book between 645 pupils. He could not thank me enough. Then he made a remark that was to become familiar all week: 'Please, please come back again. Do not forget us.'

As we pulled away, the children began singing their school song. It was something to do with education being a great victory in life. That too had a strange resonance. The books had been as important to them as food and water.

Further along, we came to Mama Beach school where the partially crippled head teacher was also struggling. In the isolated fishing village, he had over 400 pupils and just three ageing text books between them, one for maths, one for grammar and one for social studies. Not only that, one of his three blackboards was redundant. It was made from rough concrete and used a pack of chalk a day. Even that was too much for a school that was virtually penniless. He could not believe what we were doing. But he was delighted and grateful.

The following day, I made my farewells to Tenneh and left her with her social worker. Later I was to experience one of the the most moving episodes I have ever had. We loaded up the truck as usual with education supplies and headed for the Waterloo refugee camp, north of the city. Here, 12,000 people were living in mud huts after fleeing the rebels who had burned their homes and slaughtered many of their friends and relatives. The school there was one of the most deprived of all. With well over 1,000 pupils, it did not have a single book and there was even a waiting list because of a shortage of space and chairs. As we handed over books to the delighted headmaster, Daniel Williams, his daughter Emma, aged nine, appeared. She was slightly built with her hair tied in bobs. She was polite and had a painfully shy smile. What I noticed next was that her right hand was missing. Her father explained:

'Four years ago, the rebels attacked our village and we all scattered. They caught Emma, who was only five, held her hand over a tree stump and cut it off with a machete. She was then told to go. Nothing else was said.

'For 12 days she wandered alone in the bush, bleeding and in agony, eating plants and berries, until she was found by a hunter who took her to the Ecomog forces. They drove her to Freetown where she was treated at the Connaught Hospital. We were reunited when we arrived in Freetown and have ended up here, frightened to return.'

She was not alone. The camp had 210 men, women and children who had had limbs cut off as a terror warning to others. Korie Samara was a more recent victim. At eleven years old, his left hand was still bandaged after an attack just a month ago which had left his small face frozen in a staring mask of horror.

Before we left, I ensured that Emma and her sisters were given a selection of books to match their ages. She tried to turn the pages of one large picture book with her remaining hand. But it was difficult. She smiled with embarrassment as I helped her. I fought back the tears, not because of what had happened, but because this shy young girl was coping with such dignity and without the stain of hatred in her heart for a world that had been so cruel.

Next day I returned. This time I brought my good friend Adrian Horn, a former senior police officer in England who was helping to rebuild Sierra Leone's devastated civilian force.

The camp children were in church, but they poured out and we deluged them with balloons we had brought. Their priest, Father Boa Maurice, an Italian catholic father, greeted us warmly, despite our interruption of his service.

He then told me of the latest horror. A ten-year-old girl had been brought to his house the previous night. Rebels had gouged out her right eye and killed her parents. His smile vanished as he told me: 'It is done to make panic, but no words can describe what these people are doing.'

The girl would be flown to Italy for medical help, he said. And some day, God would judge her tormentors.

With a heavy heart, we bade him farewell and said we had a delivery to make. We stopped when we reached the Williams hut. Outside, Emma was surrounded by a small group, still reading the books we had delivered. Her father came out and greeted us. We opened the rear of the truck and handed over a large sack of rice. We knew how desperate the family was for food. It was a small gesture, but something we wanted to do. As we rounded the turn, I looked back. Emma was waving. She was also smiling that shy smile.

As we passed through the main camp gates, there was panic. Even there, people were not safe. There had been small raids in the past. And once again the rebels were closing fast. People were catching rides into the city, moving their possessions to relative safety. The nightmare was returning.

As I left for home the next day in a small plane bouncing along the tarmac at Hastings, I wondered at such cruelty in a land of such kindness and beauty.

I wondered if the small things we had done would make a difference. Would the children of today have different values to the men in the bush.

Would they remember one thing above all else. That one day they were touched by the kindness of a stranger?

EPILOGUE

You may give them your love but not your thoughts.
For they have their own thoughts.
You may house their bodies but not their souls,
For their souls dwell in the house of tomorrow, which you cannot visit,
Not even in your dreams.

Kahlil Gibran (1883–1931) Lebanese mystic and poet. The Prophet, 'On Children'

The nightmare *did* return to haunt orphan Tenneh Cole and amputee Emma Williams.

As if they had not suffered enough in their young lives, long days of fears and tears came back with a vengeance.

For Emma, the terror came when her parents loaded up the family's few belongings and they all fled the refugee camp that had been home for four years.

They were just in time. The rebels poured into the Waterloo camp soon after they left. The place was deserted. The Williams family had been amongst almost 12,000 displaced men, women and children who had left in the night.

For the nine-year-old with the shy smile, life was going to be hard on the run with just one arm and that little blue rucksack to carry.

I wondered if she and her sisters had managed to save their Sunday-best dresses and the books I had given them. But the books would be of little concern when matters of life and death were ahead of them. I also pictured the face of that other refugee, Korie Samara, the eleven-year-old whose arm had so recently been hacked off. He had had trouble smiling ever since. On the road once more, I imagined he would never smile again.

What, too, I wondered, had happened to the ten-year-old girl who had been taken to Father Maurice at the camp with her right eye gouged out. Would she also be fleeing for her life?

Such were the unspoken questions for which I knew there would never be answers. Such children and their individual tragedies were unlikely to be recorded by anyone in a land where the aid agencies and most foreign journalists had fled.

One mental tragedy that I was able to record was that involving Tenneh. It began in the heat of the night as she lay in bed in Freetown. It lasted for fourteen days. And only time will tell what scars it has left on her already traumatised young mind.

The rebels who attacked the refugee camp went on a rampage in Freetown, freely killing and maiming opponents and civilians alike, and burning huge swathes of the poorer eastern suburbs as well as some of the city centre's major buildings.

I had long harboured grave doubts about the ability of the overstretched Nigerian-led defenders, Ecomog, to hold back the rebels. On the day I left in a small plane from the airstrip at Hastings, a few kilometres northeast of the city, I could hear the Nigerian artillery pounding rebel bush bases just down the road. Crowds of refugees were heading for the perceived safety of Freetown's great urban sprawl. Panic was in the air. The plain-clothes Kamajor security men were beating people at roadblocks, adding to the air of impending disaster. I felt, as I always felt on such occasions, like a deserter, one of the privileged few, making my escape as the fires descended on the helpless. It would have been futile and probably fatal to have stayed behind.

Such concerns troubled me as I bade farewell to Larry Hollingworth at the airstrip. I had spent the past two days with the former Sarajevo UN aid chief. His mission was to check out the whole Hope and Homes operation in Sierra Leone and he was staying a few days longer. I knew he was vastly experienced in troublespots, but I feared for the man with the bushy white hair and beard – they had nicknamed him Father Christmas in Freetown – as the storm clouds gathered.

It was no surprise when, just a few days after arriving back in England, I learned that the rebels had swept into Freetown, forcing Ecomog back to a desperate defence line in the western area and around the main airport at Lungi.

Caught in the middle in the Congo Town district were Tenneh and her guardian. Dr Roland Kargbo, the charismatic and highly skilled founder of the orphanage charity HANCI had learned of the attack from a specialist news website on the Internet and rang Roland immediately at the single-storey house he shared with his wife and three children. I knew them all as a kind and caring family with strong religious principles.

It was one of the most disturbing telephone calls I have ever experienced in a lifetime of many disturbing calls. I was surprised that the telephone rang immediately and my international call was answered. Even in times of peace this is regarded as a minor miracle even on local calls in the country. Roland sounded breathless. He was whispering, his voice controlled and articulate but drowned out by loud crashes in the background. The noises soon became clearer, more definite, unmistakable. This was heavy-calibre machine gun fire, its staccato thumping interrupted by bursts from rifles and the occasional distant explosion. It was terrifying to hear it so clearly, knowing that the family and Tenneh were trapped there. I knew how the rebels had killed, raped and maimed people at random during their last reign in Freetown. There had also been many deaths and major destruction when Ecomog had forced them back into the bush eventually.

Roland never exaggerated. I had always found him impressively well informed and accurate in his assessments of the country's true security position. His network of contacts kept the respected academic up-to-date. And he always appeared unflappable. Even so, the scene he described stunned me completely.

'It is terrible here. There is a lot of shooting outside and I am lying here with Tenneh and my family under a bed, praying we will survive. I have with me my wife Agnes, my daughters Ria, 13, and Joy, 18, and my son Jan, who is 16. It is difficult to keep them from crying and fearing the worst. It is very hard to keep quiet for long hours with all the noise, the danger and the heat. Tenneh is playing with her toys and is being quite good. She does not really understand what is happening and she cannot really hear all the noise. My children know and are frightened. They have seen it all before.

'There is so much shooting which started at 2 a.m. at the east end of town and has spread to the centre. We have a little food, which we intend to eat sparingly and water is still running from the taps. But the shooting is very heavy, especially when the Ecomog jets come over and the machine guns open up. There is no bombing from the Alpha jets yet, but it may start if they get close to the president, who we understand is back in town, or to some of the key installations, like the Sierra Leone Broadcasting station.

'The rebels have taken over one of the small private radio stations, 96.2 FM, and have warned everyone to stay inside their homes. If anyone goes outside it will be at their own risk. They have also warned that there will be severe consequences for anyone found shielding Ecomog soldiers ... (at this stage gunfire broke into the call).

'... I have had phone calls from friends who say the rebels have already taken the prison and released all the prisoners. The streets are completely empty and everyone is hiding. If Ecomog do not do something quickly, then all is lost. The night will be horrific, the worst you can imagine. We all remember the last time, eleven months ago, when the rebels were in power. It was terrible for pro-government activists … (Gunfire again broke into Dr Kargbo's description.)

'… My fear now is also for the children at the home in Makeni. We sent two messengers there and they have disappeared. But refugees have told us that the orphans have fled back into a safe place in the bush with Peter Brymer (their manager) and the home may be being used as a rebel base.

'In the city our hopes lie with Ecomog regrouping across the river at Lungi (near the international airport) and counter-attacking. They have tanks and heavy weapons. But will it happen?

'We just do not know what the future holds. We are all praying. We knew there were many more rebels, many thousands, and that the foreign diplomats were underestimating their strength.

'Please try to bring our plight to everyone's attention. We are very frightened for the children and ourselves …'

At that point the line broke, leaving me horrified at the plight of Roland and the children. I grabbed a very strong coffee and began passing Roland's telephone number around the media, including the BBC and ITN. A live broadcast of such an interview could only help to convey the desperation of the country. I also began a series of articles on the situation over the following week. Many people rang to express their horror after reading all the joyous coverage of my reunion with Tenneh and the distribution of our donated books to the amputee children. My film report had been broadcast on Sky News as a Christmas special and a feature had been carried in the *Mail on Sunday*.

Then, exactly two weeks after contact was lost, I was back on the restored telephone line to Roland, who reported that Ecomog had, indeed, counter-attacked and were forcing back the rebels and everyone in his home was safe.

Terrified Tenneh was also alive after another near-miraculous escape in her eight years of life. Roland had invited many local people to shelter in his small home during the violence. They had lived and slept in whatever space was available as mortars and cannon fire had torn apart surrounding houses. Roland was bursting with relief. But his description was shocking:

'It is hard to believe that we are alive. But Tenneh, my wife and family, have now lived through the worst experience of our lives, thank God.

'The fighting has been horrendous. You risked almost certain death if you went outside where the rebels were fighting Ecomog with mortars, Kalashnikovs, heavy machine guns and general small arms. 'For the first seven days, we did not go out at all. All my neighbours were frightened of the bombing and came to me for refuge. We had over 50 people here for much of that time in my small house. 'Men, women and small children were sleeping where they could find a space. We stocked up with some rice, but it meant just a small handful once a day and a little water because that was off and on during the day.

'The children were terrified. Tenneh hid under a bed and my own children said she understood what was happening because she cried whenever heavy mortar or artillery shells landed nearby. The nights were awful, many of the young ones cried continually in their mother's arms. I have never been so frightened in my life. To have all these people to look after was a heavy responsibility.

'The nearest we came to death was when a mortar bomb landed on a tailor's shop, about five metres from the house. The shop was burned down and the old man inside lost a foot. We tried to get medical help, but there was no hope and he died in the night.

'We have been able to get out a little today and the scenes are terrible. Just down the road, at the roundabout, there are thirty-five bodies lying on the ground, mostly young people slaughtered by one side or another. 'There has been a great deal of panic and people who have been unable to identify themselves, particularly young men, have been shot.

'At the bridge over the main road, there have been over five hundred executions of this kind. Young men have been taken there, shot and thrown over into the river.

'Both sides appear to have carried out such executions. There has also been major destruction, whenever the rebels have put up firm resistance. Ecomog has answered this by calling in a jet which has dropped a few bombs and set fire to many homes and other properties.

'Our fear now is the rebels will become even more violent as they leave the city and head out into the country.

'We are trying to get back to some form of normality. But Tenneh and the other children will be suffering terrible psychological problems from these recent experiences. It has been the most frightening thing I have ever witnessed in my life.'

As the largely Nigerian-led Ecomog forces began to ease the rebels eastward and through the devastated poorer suburbs of Kissy, the full picture of the horror began to emerge. Roland's heroism had saved many lives. Outside, the streets were littered with bodies, rotting in the heat of the dry season and bringing rumours of cholera. The fighting had left at least 4000 dead in the streets, rivers and floating in the bays. Out to sea, bodies were seen close to the grey metal edifice of HMS Norfolk, the British frigate which had been sent to offer humanitarian assistance.

Another near-miracle was to emerge a few days later. Mark Cook rang me to say he had had confirmation that the orphans from Makeni had escaped again without death or injury. HANCI staff had rented three trucks and driven them from the bush north to a hall at Kamikwae, where ninety youngsters were being cared for and Mark was arranging emergency cash payments to provide food, medicine and other supplies. Larry Hollingworth had also managed to fly out in the nick of time.

The future looked bleak for as many as one and a half million Sierra Leoneans who had been uprooted and left without food or shelter by the fighting. Not only that, a political solution looked a distant hope. And militarily, there were growing calls in Nigeria to bring their troops home, leaving Freetown fatally exposed in the face of burgeoning rebel forces, re-equipping with the resources of the occupied diamond fields to finance them.

It was a depressing prognosis. But then that is the nature of civil wars. The children we had helped had all been saved. Mark and Caroline were determined to rehouse them if necessary. They would not be giving up on them. Nor would we.

One day I hoped to be able to deliver books to them in Makeni, as I had pledged. I had a foolish dream that this would happen in a land where everyone had food, water and shelter and a government that would give them a fair share of its wealth, including a proper health and education system.

I also hoped the children would live long enough to be adopted into loving new homes with parents who would cherish them.

Then, in February, I was asked to take part in an episode of television's *This is your Life* in honour of Mark and his work with the orphans. Tributes poured in from well known figures, including Lord Carrington, Paddy Ashdown and Martin Bell. Two teenage girls had also been flown in from Mark's first home in Lipik. They had been small children when I had last seen them there, soon after their original home had been blown up by the rampaging Bosnian Serbs.

Now they were almost young women, bright, cheerful and optimistic.

Self-consciously in the manner of all teenagers, one said simply to Mark: 'Thank-you for giving us hope, a home and a future.'

They had not found loving parents and a house and garden to call their own. It was unlikely now that they ever would. Teenagers rarely find adoptive parents. But, after the cruelty and horrors they had experienced in their young lives, they had their own rooms, their clothes, their books, their hopes and dreams.

Like Tenneh and Emma and Admir, a stranger had come into their lives and shown them a certain kindness for a time.

And they had remembered.

Maybe they always would. It was my only real hope. Nothing more. Just that.

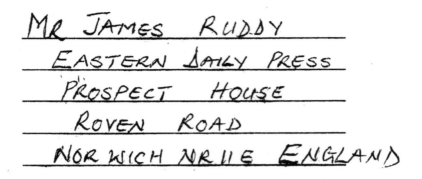

MR JAMES RUDDY
EASTERN DAILY PRESS
PROSPECT HOUSE
ROVEN ROAD
NORWICH NR11E ENGLAND

10 – 2 – 99

Dear Mr James,

I am very sorry to write you late, this is due to the many troubles and mayhem we had went through this ten months. We had been in serious problems with the R.U.F/AFRC rebels since you left us in the camp. The rebels dislodged us from the camp since the 10th of December. We travelled through the bushes by the sea side. We reached Freetown on the 13th December after three days of total sufferings in the bushes. In Freetown, we stayed with my in-laws at Calaba town in the east end of Freetown. We spent three weeks at Calaba town when the RUF/AFRC rebels dislodge a heavy attack through the hills to the city on the 6th of January at about 2 o clock mid night. They caused dismay, captured and kill innocent civilian in the city and mostly at Calaba town. My wife, Alimatu and Mayeali, my second daughter were captured that night at about 4:30 pm in the morning hours and up to this time I have not set eyes on them. Only God knows their present situation. In the intream I managed to escape with my two daughters, Emma and Zainab.

Mr James, I am please to inform you that I am presently living in paradox with my family. I am at present staying at the National Stadium. We are purely living in food scraps. The condition at the Stadium is very bad. No food supply, no proper medication and of cause we sleep in the open. Our house has been burnt down with all my belongings. Needless to talk about my children. They are always in trouble with cold and malaria. Because of the present situation I have not been able to buy them clothing. I shall send you a picture of this in my next letter, when the road to Calaba town is open.

Any way there are quite a lot I wanted to say, but all will be said in my next letter.

Extend my sincere greetings to your family and friends. A very special greetings from me, Emma and Zainab.

Mr James, you can use the above address for the main time until I will be able to locate my self.

Ta – Ta

Daniel

NB. Please dont be surprise to hear that my house in the Camp has been burnt down also.

MR DANIEL A. Y. WILLIAMS
C/O SHECK ISSA SESAY
AL-FAJR ISLAMIC MISSION
36 GODE-RICH STREET
FREE TOWN — WEST AFRICA

WITH THANKS

Without the generous support of so many, nothing of what was achieved would have been possible. The following list is by no means an exhaustive record of the financial and physical assistance provided by the readers of the *Eastern Daily Press* and the people, institutions and businesses of this country. To you all our heartfelt thanks, and, if you are not mentioned your contribution was no less welcome. You have truly shown '*the kindness of a stranger*'.

June, Jared and Janna Ruddy.
The readers of the *Eastern Daily Press*.
Col Mark and Caroline Cook, of Hope and Homes for Children.
Baroness Chalker.
Dr Roland Kargbo, of Help a Needy Child International.
Peter Franzen and his staff at the *Eastern Daily Press*.
Sir Timothy Colman.
Martin Bell.
Richard Drew and the nursing staff at the Norfolk and Norwich Hospital.
Liz Carlyle and Norfolk Guides.
Sarajevo String Quartet.
Col Roger Brunt. 1st Battalion Royal Anglian Regiment.
Capt. Charles Calder. 1st Battalion Royal Anglian Regiment.
Maj. Mark Wenham. 1st Battalion Royal Anglian Regiment.
James Whiting, of Hope and Homes for Children.
Larry Hollingworth.
Jean Goodman.
Anne-Marie Huby and her team at Medecins Sans Frontieres.
Allan Bardsley.
Mandy O'Toole.
Ken MacIntosh.

Per Hall.
Bill Ward.
Maureen Brown and the Bupa Norwich team.
Geoffrey Cheney.
Barbara Collins and friends.
Dick Meadows and BBC East.
Tom Stevenson.
Johnny Hustler.
Allan Waller.
Frank Rycroft and his Turners team.
Jim Watson, of Foulgers Transport.
Chris Bryant and his Regional Freight Services team.
Amir Zelic and the orphans of Sarajevo.
Goran Nikles and the orphans of Lipik.
The late Joseph Kargbo and the orphans of Makeni.
Professor David Southall and his team at the North Staffs Hospital.
Kevin McPhillips.
Ray Wilkinson and UNHCR.
Mark Hopley and his Tesco team (Blue Boar Lane, Sprowston).
Professor Nigel Osborne.
Maj. Jean Bouchard.
Adrian Horn.
Ven Tony Foottit.
Lawrie Sear.
Martin Kirby.

Dick Watts.
Dennis Whitehead.
Paul Durrant.
Alex Goodwin and her BT team.
Dr Steve Main.
Alan Dean.
Michael Nicholson.
Terry Foley and his team at McDonalds.
Pizza Express.
Michael Spurr and his staff, and inmates at Norwich Prison.
Simon Finlay.
Annette Hudson.
David Clayton and Radio Norfolk.
Dick Hutchinson and Radio Broadland.
David Jennings and Anglia Television.
Sue Wallis and her staff at the Early Learning Centre.
Roy Dowen and his staff at Lynn Starr.
David Greenacre.
Mark Lenton, Mike Strudwick and the distribution team at ECN.
Philip Barnett and the British Embassy team, Sarajevo.
Colin Glass and the British High Commission team, Freetown.
Robert Lamont and Norwich Marchesi Rotary Club.
Mark Fitzsimmons and Norwich Union.
Mike Lynn and The Stationery Office.
Andrew and Tanja Bone.
Alan Childs.
Charles Harrold and his St John's Ambulance team.
Brooke School.
Mansfields Amalgamated.
Norfolk Women's Institute.
Taverham Guides.
Norfolk Industries for the Blind.

Norwich and Peterborough Building Society.
Norman Potter.
Eileen Crisp.
Dr Walter Roy and the Hewett School.
Riddlesworth Hall School.
Glenn Burrell.
Ray Mumford.
PC Phillip Burton and his ATC team.
Barry Sillis and East Coast Warehousing.
Tim Fitzmaurice and Fitzmaurice Carriers.
Colmans of Norwich.
Nick Thompson and Thompson Packaging.
Hartismere High School.
Yarmouth High School.
Kinsale First School.
Jeyes of Thetford.
Norwich Castle Round Table.
Taverham Scouts.
West Runton Scouts.
1st Old Catton Guides.
Hethersett Women's Institute.
Godfrey DiY.
Long Stratton High School.
Mundham and Seething School.
Jarrolds Department Store.
Anglian Water.
The Post Office.
Air UK, Norwich.
Pizza Hut.
Langley School.
Matthews Norfolk Brass.
Fakenham Round Table.
Costessey Junior School.
Norwich Citadel Salvation Army.
Broadland Youth Choir.
Carbrooke School.
Broadland Youth Choir and Bel Canto.

Thanks to all those individuals and businesses across East Anglia and Britain who have helped again and again.

Many thanks to the *Eastern Daily Press* for permission to use their photographs in this book.